CANADIAN WAR POSTERS

CANADIAN
WAR POSTERS

1914-1918
1939-1945

MARC H. CHOKO

Méridien

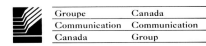

Groupe	Canada
Communication	Communication
Canada	Group

Canadian Cataloguing in Publication Data

Choko, Marc H., 1947-

Canadian War Posters : 1914-1918, 1939-1945

Issued also in french under title: Affiches de guerre
canadiennes.
Co-published by: Groupe Communication Canada.
Includes bibliographical references.

ISBN 0-929058-04-6

1. World War, 1914-1918 - Canada - Posters.   2. World
War, 1939-1945 - Canada - Posters.   War posters, Canadian.
I. Groupe Communication Canada. II. Title.

D522.25.C46 1993   769'.49940371   C94-940088-2

Cover : Details of colour plate XVII
Design : Marc H. Choko

Available in Canada through your local bookseller
or by mail from Canada Communication Group – Publishing
Ottawa, Canada K1A 0S9
Catalogue No. P60 - 4/8 - 1993E

© Éditions du Méridien, 1994

Legal deposit 1994 — Bibliothèque nationale du Québec

Printed in Canada

For Michèle

CONTENTS

ACKNOWLEDGMENTS

Many people helped me produce this book, both supplying information and finding illustrations.

In particular, I would like to thank Jim Burant, Sylvie Gervais, Kate O'Rourke, and Micheline Robert, Documentary Art and Photography Division, National Archives of Canada; Hugh A. Halliday, curator of photographs and posters, Canadian War Museum; Gary Tynski, assistant curator, and Bruce Whiteman, curator, Rare Books and Special Collections, McGill University; Bernard Lutz, archivist, National Film Board; Richard C. Allen, the Carson Collection; Maurice Doll, curator of Government History, Alberta Historical Resources; David L. Jones, Public Relations, Canadian Pacific; Janice Rosen, manager of the Archives, Canadian Jewish Congress; and Robert Stacey, researcher and author.

I am very grateful to the following, who generously gave of their time for very enlightening interviews: Roger Couillard (1989), Henri Eveleigh (1986 and 1992), Allan Harrison (1985) and Harry Mayerovitch (1992). They were extremely helpful in specifying various aspects of poster production and the role of graphic designers during the Second World War.

This publication received a grant from the *Service des publications du vice-rectorat aux communications*, Université du Québec à Montréal.

The spirit of a country is reflected in the creative expression of its people, and the posters reproduced in this book depict one such aspect of this expression. Besides evoking the flavour of the time, i believe that these posters are signposts to the efforts canadians had to make in order to mobilise for war.

One of Canada's foremost historians describes Canada's history, since Confederation in 1867, as the age of conflict. These have been two global wars in the twentieth century, and in both of these wars Canada mobilised virtually all the country's resources to meet its alliance commitments. It was a painful way for a young country to come of age, but the experience proved the enduring quality of our people and our institutions.

I find it amazing that during the Great War of 1914-18, from a population of about eight million, this country managed to raise an army of over 600,000, a navy of 9,600 personnel and 115 vessels, and sent more than twenty thousand young men to serve in the British flying services, as well as over 3,000 nursing sisters with the medical corps. What was more shocking was the cost in human lives. The worst example was in the Canadian Expeditionary Force overseas. Of 419,485 soldiers in the Canadian Corps — the largest active army formation ever to have been organised by Canada — about 60,000 died, a fatality rate of 14,2 per cent. When casualties rose to extreme levels, the government introduced conscription, a move that led to severe unrest and nearly undermined national unity in 1917-18.

Many of us are not aware that Canada's industrial effort in the First Wold War was extraordinary for such a small country so far from fields of war. The Imperial Munitions Board co-ordinated contracts in Canada worth more than a billion dollars, and established seven new "national factories" to produce war materiel. Canadian Aeroplanes Limited, for example produced about 2,900 training aircraft, and by the end of the war was also producing about eight flying boats a month for the US Navy. Canadian shipyards produced merchant ships, small patrol vessels for anti-submarines for the Royal Navy. Our country raised one and three quarters billion dollars by the sale of bonds in "Victory Loan" campaigns and through the Canadian Patriotic Fund.

In the Second World War Canada responded just as vigorously. We can be proud that, as Canadians, we were again willing to stand up and be counted, despite the dreadful losses of 1914-18. Our population had reached the eleven million mark. There were about two and a half million men between the ages of 18 and 45. More than a million of them, together with about fifty thousand women, served in uniform.

The war effort in the Second World War was at once more widespread geographically and proportionately less costly in human lives than that of the First World War. In spite of fears that overseas commitments would once again undermine national unity, the army played a major role in the European war. A Canadian Corps fought its way from Sicily to northern Italy from 1943 to 1945, and Canada had an Army in the field for the first time during the north-west European campaigns of 1944-45. The navy expanded from 1,500 men and 11 fighting ships to about 100,000 men and women and well over 350 ships. We must also not forget that thousands of Canadian merchant mariners sailed under the most hasardous conditions to carry people and goods to and from the theatres of war. The airforce, besides running the British Commonwealth Air Training Plan in Canada (a schema that produced 131,553 aircrew), expanded from about 1,200 personnel and 53 largely out-of-date aircrafts to over 220,000 men and women and a total of 70 squadrons, 48 of them overseas. We still paid a price for our participation; in the Second World War over 43,000 Canadians lost their lives.

The Second World War, following upon the moribund years of the Great Depression, introduced a new era in Canadian industry. The value of Canadian production between 1939 and 1945 was about 10 billion dollars. It was a credit to our automotive industry in 1942 that virtually all trucks supplied to the British Eighth Army in North Africa were from Canada. In 1944, the peak year, Canadian factories turned out 4,178 aircrafts. Shipyards, in their peak year of 1943, completed 150 merchant ships; in 1944 they built 73 escorts, 59 weepers and 1,953 landing crafts. The general population, through nine Victory Loans in the Second World War, raised twelve billion dollars.

The two world wars were important moments in the transition of Canada from colony to nation. Many of the posters in this collection not only accompanied and ornamented these achievement but, in a real sense, helped make them possible.

Robert R. Fowler
National Defense Headquarters

FOREWORD

In 1986, when I curated the exhibition *150 ans de graphisme publicitaire au Québec* for the *Centre de design* at Université du Québec à Montréal, I devoted a good deal of space to posters from the two world wars. There were a number of reasons for this. The First World War played a decisive role in poster development in Canada. The massive utilization, larger formats, variety, and quality of the posters produced brought this type of advertising, which had lagged behind Europe's, into the modern era. As well, Canadian war posters, which compare favourably to those produced in the United States, Great Britain, and France, have been almost totally ignored in the many books that have been written on the subject. Finally, the juxtaposition of posters from the world wars, which have been preserved in great numbers in collections across Canada, illustrates many aspects of our history.

Les Éditions du Méridien had planned to publish this book in 1989—well timed, I felt, to coincide with the seventy-fifth and fiftieth anniversaries, respectively, of the beginning of the world wars. Unfortunately, however, the project had to be postponed, and many people have been eagerly awaiting its publication.

To date, apart from a few passing mentions, only Robert Stacey, in *100 Years of the Poster in Canada*, devoted any substantial space to these war posters. However, he was able to include only a limited number of them; as well, he provided little information on their production, and none at all on the artists.

It was thus with great pleasure that I got to work when the decision was made to publish this book. I trust that it will meet expectations, do justice to the artists who designed these remarkable posters, and be of value to everyone who is interested in this area.

1.

The context for posters was very different in each of the two world wars. At the time the First World War broke out, the main means of communication in Canada was the newspaper. Posters were used for advertising—in fact, much more widely than is generally thought—but nowhere near as massively as they had been used in Europe since the late nineteenth century.

When Great Britain declared war on Germany, on August 4, 1914, the Dominion of Canada de facto found itself at war in support of the mother country, whose actions it imitated. But Canada was still a young, growing country, with a constant influx of new immigrants. The provinces jealously guarded their powers, limiting those of the central government.

Posters grew in importance thanks to initiatives by various levels of government, donations by private companies and individuals, and decisions by commanders of various recruitment units. Propaganda techniques were not highly developed, the messages not well controlled, and the imagery often naïve. Nevertheless, the posters of the First World War perfectly illustrate all aspects of the formidable effort that Canada devoted to the conflict, showed how Canadian society was evolving and the tensions that ran through it, and marked the progress of the war to its conclusion.

When the Second World War was set off by German troops marching into Poland on September 1, 1939, newspapers were still the dominant form of communication in Canada. However, radio was making great inroads, newsreels ran before every feature film, and advertising campaigns using posters were proliferating. The federal government felt that it had to centralize information control and undertake a

propaganda campaign to increase public acceptance of a new war effort. The tools and structures of this centralization came into existence over time. Enormous quantities of posters, in addition to the many other means of mass communication, spread the wartime slogans urging young men to enlist, women to go out and get jobs, and everyone to save, to give financial support, to salvage materials essential to war production, to mistrust the enemy, and so on.

During both world wars, the huge number of posters produced created tremendous business for the large printing companies and for graphic designers. Some of the latter were artists who wanted to serve their country. Many were professional graphic artists, making a living through "commercial art" and putting their expertise at the service of the two most important poster campaigns in the history of Canada.

Canadian war posters were usually literal and narrative, combining figurative illustration and text. Many were inspired by—sometimes even copied or adapted from—posters produced by the Allies, but some were beautiful, and unjustly ignored works.

Among the thousands of posters produced during the two wars, I had to make choices. I want to provide a look at the different graphic styles through the works I feel are the best, and also give an overview of all the aspects of the genre that deserve to be exemplified.

3.

ALLONS-Y

Hilcox.

BLIÉE PAR LE SERVICE DE L'INFORMATION, AVEC L'AUTORISATION DE L'HON J. T. THORSON, MINISTRE DES SERVICES NATIONAUX DE GUERRE, OTTAWA   IMPRIMÉE AU CANADA   UF 4E

4.

A LONG WAR IN THE TRENCHES

In August, 1914, Canada, along with the other countries in the British Empire, found itself at war. Given the alliances of the time, two sides were formed: the German and Austro-Hungarian empires on one; Great Britain, France, Russia, and Serbia on the other. Strangely, the atmosphere everywhere was almost festive: overestimating the strength and preparedness of their troops, both sides thought that the war would be over quickly. The soldiers marched off with a light step.

In Canada, a vast majority supported the idea of participating in the war effort. Sir Robert Laird Borden's Conservative government received the support of Sir Wilfrid Laurier's Liberal opposition; even Henri Bourassa's French-Canadian nationalists declared themselves in favour of participation. The War Measures Act gave the federal government the power to do what was needed: recruit volunteers, raise funds, boost industrial and agricultural production, and so on.

The first eighteen thousand Canadian troops landed in Saint-Nazaire, France, on February 12, 1915, and were sent to the northern front, between Dunkirk and Arras, not far from the Belgian border, under British command. For two months, the Canadian soldiers sat quietly south of Armentières. Then they were moved to an almost unprotected line of trenches—few sandbags, shallow trenches—at Ypres, between the French and English troops, and were not even issued steel helmets. They underwent a baptism by fire on April 22, 1915, and the shock was brutal. The intense German artillery fire, laying the ground for infantry attacks, and especially the surprise use of poison gas caused enormous losses among the Canadian troops. In less than one week of combat, 1,988 soldiers were

5.

6.

ARTILLERY
HEROES AT THE FRONT
SAY
"GET INTO A MAN'S UNIFORM"

APPLY
BASE RECRUITING DEPÔT
SPARKS ST.
OTTAWA   ONTARIO

7.

killed and 4,116 were injured among the First Division and the Prince Patricia's Canadian Light Infantry. Thereafter, the names "Saint-Julien" and "Langemarck" would be symbols of Canadian soldiers' heroism, immortalized in many posters.

One year later, it was the Second Division, sent to the front to replace exhausted English troops, that suffered a murderous German attack at Saint-Eloi. On June 2, 1916, an incessant barrage of shelling devastated the Third Division's trenches at Mont Sorrel; the commandant, General Mercer, was killed, as were many of the soldiers holding the position. Throughout the summer, three Canadian divisions relieved each other on the front in the Bapaume region. In September, they took part in the Battle of the Somme, where tanks were used for the first time; supported by English and Canadian artillery fire, they took their first positions. The battle raged throughout the autumn. There were now four Canadian divisions fighting alongside the Allied troops. Better equipped, more war-hardened, and also better led (the first defeats at least got rid of some of the most incompetent officers), they took part in the victories of the end of November. Among the Canadians alone, the battles of the Somme resulted in more than twenty-four thousand men dead, wounded, or missing.

On April 9, 1917, it was on Vimy Ridge, said to be impregnable, that the Canadian soldiers of the four divisions gained their renown. After careful preparations, the digging of eleven approach tunnels, and an artillery barrage, the ridge was taken, though not without heavy losses: 3,598 dead and 7,004 wounded.

Festubert, Givenchy, and many other place names were added to the already long list celebrating the great feats of Canadian troops.

After three years of hard combat under exhausting conditions, everyone knew that this was what making war really meant. The party had turned into a nightmare. There were always more recruits needed to fill the gaps, hold the trenches, launch fresh offensives. The war was expanded to new regions, then into the sea and the air.

Now, the posters showed the trenches, the shells exploding, the wounded, even the dead. The appeals were more urgent. Although some posters still had an enthusiastic tone, it was obvious that the situation was

8.

9.

grave: the troops on the Russian front were in retreat, the French army was on the verge of mutiny, and German submarines had established an almost hermetic blockade of Great Britain. Those who feared the worst were right: it was indeed yet to come. On the morning of October 26, 1917, when the Canadian troops were forced to follow up the British offensive on Passchendaele, their victory was once again terribly bitter, with 15,654 dead and wounded in just a few days. The unprecedented massacre had been predicted by Lieutenant-General Arthur Currie, who nevertheless was constrained to obey orders. Unfortunately, the costly victory did not change the course of the war.

Everywhere, the Allies went down to defeat. In March, 1918, the German army, led by von Hindenburg and Ludendorff, reinforced by liberated troops from the Russian front after the Revolution and the signing of a peace treaty on December 15, 1917, launched a vast general offensive that continued until July. Marshal Foch, named in March to head all the Allied armies, managed to repel the German attack on the Somme in April, 1918. In July, he won the second battle of the Marne; backed by the reinforcements that were starting to pour in, notably those of the American expeditionary force following the United States' entry into the war, he launched a general offensive. On August 8, near Amiens, the Canadians, fighting alongside the Australians, wiped out the German lines with a combined tank, infantry, and air-assault attack. The Canadian troops, with the other Allied forces, continued to push ahead; finally, the Germans retreated on all fronts, and the armistice was signed on November 11, 1918.

Among the Canadian expeditionary forces, 60,661 soldiers lost their lives out of the more than 400,000 who took part in the combat, and many more went home permanently maimed, shell-shocked, or traumatized.

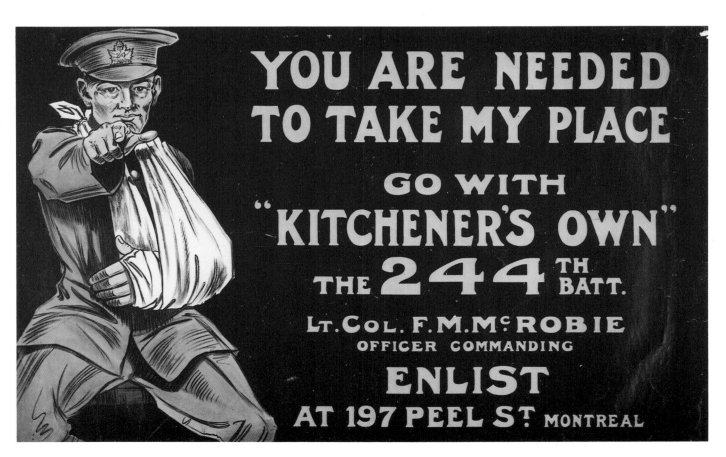

10.

12.

THE BLITZKRIEG

On September 1, 1939, the Germans invaded Poland and launched blitzkriegs combining tanks, motorized troops, and airplanes. This time, Great Britain and France entered the war because of existing alliance treaties. The Canadian Liberal government, led by William L. Mackenzie King, had applauded Neville Chamberlain's retreat when Czechoslovakia was invaded. Now, however, King had to keep his promise and fight alongside his allies. Canada declared war on September 10, 1939; the opposition in parliament voted with the government, but on the basis of an agreement that there would be no conscription for overseas service.

Everyone thought that Canada's war effort would be limited to financial and industrial support, especially since the western front was calm. Belgium and the Netherlands had declared themselves neutral and refused the preventive advance of English troops. The French were holding the Maginot Line, thought to be impenetrable. As the "strange war" proceeded, the English and French stood by while Poland was divided between Germany and Russia, which had gone to war on September 18. The Russians also attacked Finland, then swept through the Baltic states. On April 9, 1940, German troops seized Denmark and Norway. Then, in May, Belgium and the Netherlands surrendered. A tank blitzkrieg by General Guderian through the Ardennes (the Battle of the Bulge), covered by a masterful air force, swept away all French resistance and forced a hurried exodus of populations and the retreat toward England of more than three hundred thousand English and French soldiers surrounded at Dunkirk.

Marshal Pétain, who took over as head of the French government on June 17, signed a truce on the 22nd. Hitler then began the Battle of Britain, ordering the

13.

massive bombing of maritime convoys, ports, industries, and populations. At the same time, the war was extended to Africa, where Italian troops overran Somalia, Sudan, Kenya, Ethiopia, and Libya. German troops took Yugoslavia and Greece in April, 1941. Then, breaking the secret pact signed with the USSR, a massive attack on the eastern front began on June 21, 1941: four thousand tanks and three thousand planes supported the German army, reinforced by Hungarian, Romanian, and Slovak troops, while Finnish troops rekindled the war in the north.

Up to this point, Canada witnessed the formidable war from afar, although conscription for national defence was imposed in June, 1940. The financial effort grew and industrial production was considerably expanded, but no Canadian troops were committed.

On December 7, 1941, the surprise Japanese attack on Pearl Harbor made it truly a world conflict. The United States, until then quite reluctant to join the war, now threw its entire weight in the balance on the Allied side. The Japanese continued to push into Asia, and it was in defence of Hong Kong, in December, 1941, that the first soldiers of the Canadian expeditionary corps, all volunteers, were engaged. During this time, the Canadian forces stationed in Great Britain were in training. Their first combat, at the failed landing at Dieppe, on August 12, 1942, was to be a hard awakening.

But for the moment, it was the navy, in the battle against German submarines, that was leading much of the war effort, although the air force also produced a considerable effort. The Royal Canadian Air Force ran the Commonwealth's hundred aviation schools, preparing the élite air crews that would spearhead the Allied reconquest of Europe.

The Canadian First Infantry Division participated in the landing at Sicily in July, 1943, then in the advance into Italy starting in December. Thereafter, the Allied powers took the upper hand everywhere. The Soviets, defeating the German troops at Stalingrad, precipitated Germany's retreat. The Americans took the initiative in the Pacific. The British reversed the situation in Africa. Canadian troops now numbered 92,000 in Italy, of whom 5,764 were to be killed.

The Third Division and the Second Tank Brigade participated in the landing at Normandy on June 6, 1944, under British command, and engaged in hard

14.

15.

29

combat. The Canadian First Army took a number of French coastal towns. They fought fiercely in Escaut, Belgium, then on the Rhine, and finally in the Netherlands. The cost in Canadian lives of these victorious offensives was 11,336.

Canadians also contributed heavily to the air war, notably in night bombing missions on Germany, the most dangerous. Almost 10,000 men lost their lives in this effort.

When the war came to an end on all fronts, 42,042 Canadians had died. The blitzkrieg that was to conquer the world for Hitler had lasted almost six years and cost the lives of tens of millions, an unprecedented slaughter.

Two-man boarding party from the Canadian corvette 'Oakville' subdues crew of German sub in Caribbean

16.

17.

18.

ENLIST !

When the First World War broke out, the Canadian army comprised only three thousand men, although six thousand militiamen had been trained in 1913. Sam Hughes, the minister of war, launched an appeal for volunteers. His objective of gathering twenty-five hundred men was surpassed; thirty-three hundred volunteers presented themselves at the Valcartier camp. The strong presence of many newly arrived British immigrants, the high rate of unemployment, and the promised pay stimulated this recruitment.

The Conservative prime minister, Sir Robert Borden, had promised that the government would not resort to conscription; it seemed that he would be able to keep his word. Recruitment was carried out locally, thanks for the most part to private donations, which financed poster production. The tone was usually jovial, even humorous, almost always personalized. The volunteers knew in advance in which branch and regiment they would serve and under which leaders. They also knew that they would be among men of their own background—English or French Canadians, Irish, Scottish, Jewish—and from their own region.

The imagery in the posters, often naïve, was accompanied by slogans that appealed to the pride of the volunteers. Images of the English flag and Lord Horatio Herbert Kitchener, the British war minister, were used in posters aimed at English Canadians. The posters for recruitment of French Canadians played sometimes on the feeling of belonging to a proud race, loyal to its origins, sometimes directly on links with France.

By the end of 1915, 330,000 men had volunteered. But the war dragged on, requiring more and more soldiers, claiming more and more victims. Recruitment became an increasingly urgent matter, especially since

19.

Join the Team!

ROYAL CANADIAN
AIR FORCE

TED HARRIS

20.

21.

English Canadians felt that French Canadians were not doing their part. Borden, in his 1916 New Year's message, called for half a million men to step forward, but he still did not impose conscription, because of very strong resistance from his Quebec caucus. In August of 1916, in an effort at compromise, a national registration program was instituted, but the latest attempts at recruitment in Quebec ended in failure in 1917. Meanwhile, the economic machine was running full steam ahead and both industry and agriculture were seeking workers. The law on obligatory military service, passed in August 1917, gave rise to riots in Montreal. Only 19,050 Quebecers were conscripted, and almost as many of those drafted refused to present themselves or managed to make use of the many exemptions.

During the entire period of the First World War, 257 infantry battalions were raised across Canada, including 95 in Ontario and 87 in the western provinces; Quebec supplied only 20. Some of the battalions comprised particular corps, such as cavalry, artillery, rail transport, or the forestry corps. At the same time, the navy was proceeding with its own recruitment effort, while a handful of Canadians enlisted for the Royal Air Force.

In spite of all the harbingers, the Canadian armed forces, again consisting entirely of volunteers, were no better prepared when the Second World War began. At the end of 1939, there were only forty-five hundred men in the ground forces, four thousand in the air force, and seventeen hundred in the the navy, and equipment was very limited. The navy had only fifteen vessels, six of them battleships.

Again, the prime minister, this time William L. Mackenzie King, a Liberal, promised that there would be no conscription for overseas service. But in June, 1940, the National Resources Mobilization Act imposed conscription for interior defence. This time, recruitment of volunteers was planned on a national scale by the federal government. Posters were addressed to all Canadians and, with few exceptions, the same illustrations were used with different English and French texts. The texts themselves had been reduced to brief slogans. The Canadian army, like the country, was to be unified. Again, however, voluntary enlistment was low in Quebec compared to other

22.

23.

37

provinces. Even in English Canada, there was little enthusiasm for conscription and overseas service.

In spite of this, the Canadian armed forces had grown considerably by the end of 1943. The ground army comprised 460,000 men, including three infantry divisions and two combat tank divisions, along with communications, repair, and supply sections and a large reserve army. There were more than two hundred thousand people in the air force, and they fought beside the Americans in the Pacific and within the Royal Air Force in Europe. The Canadians were also in charge of the Commonwealth air force training programme, and trained valuable, courageous pilots who participated in the dangerous bombing missions over Germany. As for the navy, it now had 550 destroyers, frigates, corvettes, cruisers, and minesweepers, and a force of more than sixty-seven thousand men. Its regular duties included convoy protection, harbour control, minesweeping, and hunting submarines, in both the Pacific and Atlantic oceans.

However, this formidable growth in assets was deemed insufficient; in the fall of 1944, Mackenzie King, under growing pressure from his own party, finally sent a large contingent of conscripted soldiers to Europe.

24.

THE SPIRIT
OF CANADA'S
WOMEN

CANADIAN WOMEN'S ARMY CORPS

25.

26.

Come on CANADA!

27.

28.

AGAINST BARBARISM

During both world wars, Canadian territory and citizens at home were never directly affected, except for a few incidents in September, 1942, when German submarines ventured up the St. Lawrence River and sank a number of ships. First World War propaganda used the concept of not waiting until the enemy was at the door to fight him off, in order to convince volunteers to confront him on his own ground, in Europe. Posters presented the images of Montreal's Notre-Dame Cathedral on fire, Canadian houses destroyed, Canadian women and children murdered.

But these illustrations, with much less violence than in American or European posters, were the exception. As a general rule, the enemy was ridiculed and many of the posters depicting him were treated in a humorous fashion. Very few posters showed the damage and unhappiness inflicted on Allied civilians, in order to make Canadians sympathize with their suffering. One poster aimed at French Canadians appealed to Catholic values to encourage them to fight Nazi barbarism. But over all, aside from portrayals of soldiers taking part in overseas battle, the barbarism remained very abstract.

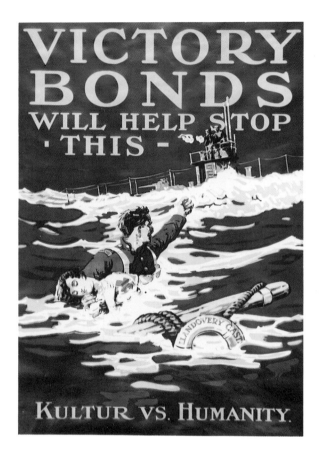

29.

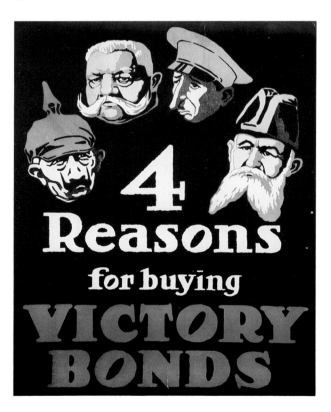

30.

31.

32.

33.

34.

35.

36.

GIVE YOUR GOLD

Recruiting men, always more men, to fight the enemy was an essential task. But on top of this, the men had to be equipped and paid a salary to provide for their families, and assistance had to be sent to the Allies. Money became a crucial problem, and new ways had to be found to amass ever larger sums. Canada began by appealing for donations, then for voluntary thrift, and finally turned to imposing taxes.

At the beginning of the First World War, donations enabled various regiments to conduct their local recruiting campaigns. But the funds gathered this way fell far short of filling the needs of a wartime army consisting of hundreds of thousands of men. After securing a loan from the United States, in 1915, Thomas White, the minister of finance, asked Canadians to help with the war effort by purchasing government bonds. A hundred million dollars' worth of "victory bonds" were issued and rapidly bought up. Each soldier's family received a monthly stipend of between twenty and sixty dollars, depending on the soldier's rank. New bond issues were also made in 1916 ($100 million), 1917 ($139 million and $398 million), and 1918 ($660 million).

At the same time, the government raised import duties; in 1916, it taxed corporate profits; finally, in April of 1917, it decided to impose a war tax on personal income, which was to stop as soon as the war ended. From 1913 to 1918, Canada's debt went from .5 to 2.5 billion dollars, underlining the gigantic effort devoted to the war.

The figures were even higher during the Second World War. The expenses side of the Canadian budget in 1939–40 totalled 120 million dollars; by 1942, expenditures were approaching 4 billion, and in 1943–44 they reached 4.6 billion. Aid from Canada to

Great Britain alone surpassed 3 billion dollars, including 1 billion donated in 1942.

There were nine loans between June 1941 and October 1945, which yielded revenues almost $10 billion of Canadians' savings. But these considerable efforts were very much to the profit of Canadians. Indeed, Canada was the main supplier to the Allied forces during the First World War, and the second-largest supplier, after the United States, during the Second World War. Both industry and agriculture were working to capacity to meet the needs of the Canadian and Allied armies, notably Great Britain's. And savings accrued interest. Thus, each family that bought bonds was ensuring its future prosperity.

As the saying went, "Money is the sinews of war," and the many posters produced during the two wars bear this out. Everyone was urged to participate, according to his or her means, in the massive mobilization. Men who did not fight did their part, and employers helped out by deducting from their payrolls the sums necessary to purchase bonds. Housewives economized on their family budgets to acquire thrift stamps, which they accumulated to purchase the valuable bonds. In the end, children would be asked to do the same.

In this way, the entire nation was mobilized to arm Canada's soldiers, hasten the end of the war and their return home, and prepare for the future.

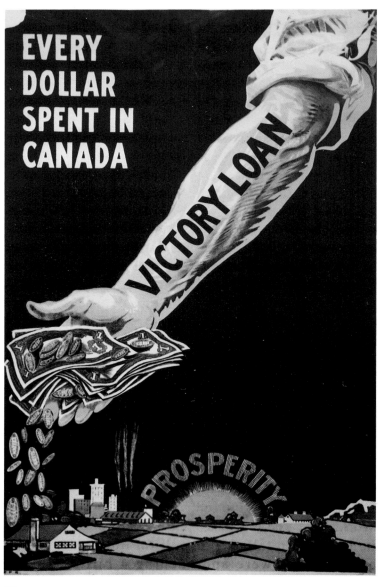

37.

39.

41.

THE WAR EFFORT

To transform a peacetime economy that was stagnant, if not in crisis, into a vast war machine, Canada had to go through a number of changes. Production in many enterprises had to be reoriented and stepped up, women entered the factories en masse, agriculture had to mobilize new workers. Salvage mechanisms for certain materials essential to war production had to be set up, and the population had to be urged not to waste. When shortages loomed on the horizon, people had to be watched and hoarders prosecuted. During the First World War, there were "meatless Fridays" and "gasless Sundays."

During the Second World War, the production effort was huge. Canada made more than eighty thousand military vehicles, among them thousands of Valentine, Ram, and M4 assault tanks. Firms that built training and combat planes expanded formidably. More than twenty thousand planes were manufactured, from Mosquito two-engine planes to giant four-engine Lancaster bombers. Shipyards launched hundreds of cargo ships, frigates, corvettes, and minesweepers. Manufacture of cannons, artillery, portable arms, and other materiel kept hundreds of factories busy and employed more than a million workers, including a quarter of a million women. Lumber, charcoal, rubber, non-ferrous metals, agriculture—all sectors of the Canadian economy saw unprecedented activity.

Second World War posters in particular portray this fraternal struggle of soldiers and workers labouring inseparably side by side. But the other basic aspect shown by many posters produced during both wars is the new role of the woman in Canadian society. In fact, I should say "roles," since there were many, from her traditional place in the home looking after thrift and salvage, to the fields, where she helped the men, to new roles in factories and the armed forces.

42.

43.

44.

45.

46.

47.

48.

49.

50.

51.

52.

When an entire country mobilizes in a gigantic war effort, more and more families weep for a lost member, and people face increasing hardships and restrictions, dissent is not long in finding fertile ground. Canadian soldiers knew the enemy they were fighting in the battlefield. But there were other enemies, hidden, silent—those within, which had to be uncovered.

Immigrants from "enemy" countries, once welcomed, such as Italians and Japanese, were arrested and placed in camps during the Second World War, as were socialists and communists after 1917 and also between 1939 and 1941, and French Canadians who were opposed to conscription and called for people to vote against the government. In turn, these groups were the object of resentment, discriminatory measures, and sometimes extortion.

Finally, during the Second World War, there was widespread paranoia about foreign spies. It must be kept in mind that since Canada was the main supplier of war materiel and supplies for the Allies, aside from the United States, and its principal role was protecting maritime convoys crossing the Atlantic, any information leaked on these convoys could mean their interception by the hordes of German submarines that ventured as far as Newfoundland and even up the St. Lawrence River.

Posters calling for prudence and discretion were printed and distributed in very large numbers, even though it was impossible to determine if there was really a need for these qualities.

54.

55.

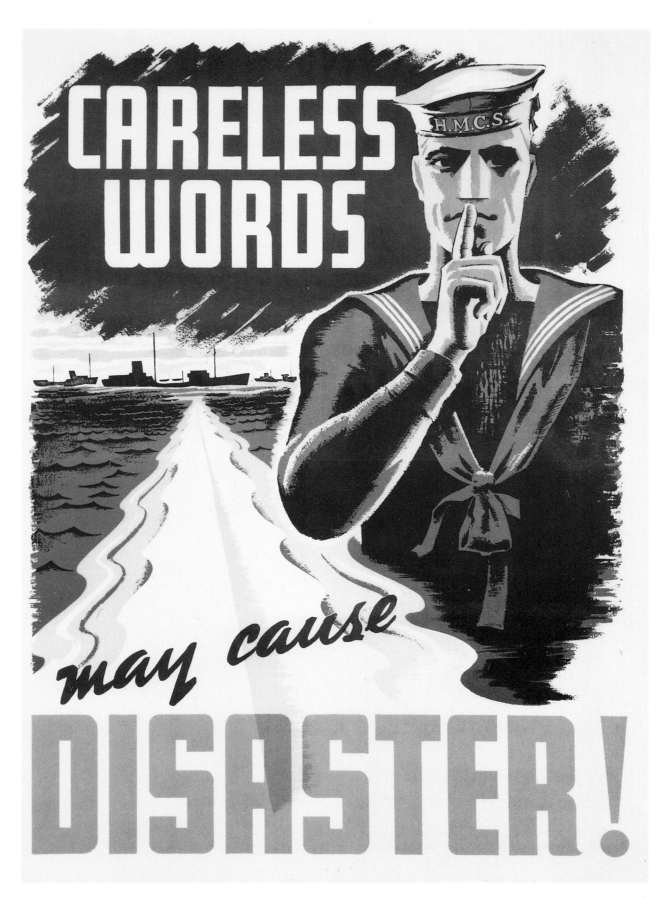

56.

CANADIENS
Suivez l'Exemple de
Dollard des Ormeaux
N'attendez pas l'ennemi au coin du feu, mais allez au devant de lui.

En Avant! Canadiens-Francais
Enrolez-vous dans les Régiments
Canadiens-Français
□□□
Adressez-vous au
Comité de Recrutement Canadien-Francais

MONTREAL,
Arsenal du 65ième Régiment,
Avenue des Pins.

QUEBEC,
Place Jacques-Cartier, coin des rues
St-François et de la Couronne.

OTTAWA,
106, rue York.

SHERBROOKE,
rue Wellington.

TROIS-RIVIERES,
71a, rue Champflour.

JOLIETTE,
110, rue Manceau.

CHICOUTIMI,
rue Racine.

57.

PRODUCTION OF
CANADIAN WAR POSTERS

Given that Canadian war posters went utterly unrecognized, and sometimes were even attributed to other nations, a number of questions are raised. Who were the artists who designed them ? Who ordered them? Was there any control over their content ? Who printed them, how, in what quantities ? And when were they made ? Unfortunately, few answers can be supplied, since many documents dealing specifically with poster production have been lost or mislaid.

During the First World War, no government agency was responsible for controlling poster production. Canada was completely inexperienced with regard to massive propaganda campaigns, even though posters had been used in federal elections. The initiatives were many and varied, coming from companies and from wealthy citizens wishing to participate in the war effort. Recruitment posters were made by individual regiments, which contacted printing companies close to their quarters. The commandant would sometimes ask for price quotations and request adjustments to the graphic design or the text. After he paid for and took delivery of the posters, he was then responsible for posting them in appropriate spots.

The quality of the posters depended, of course, on the talent of the graphic designers working at the printing companies, most of whom were accustomed to creating realistic posters to sell consumer products. Some borrowed directly from foreign works and adapted them to the situation. In some cases, the image was appropriated and reframed and a different text was added, as in the poster for recruitment for the 69th Artillery Division and the one appealing to women to serve their country. In other cases, the idea was retained and new images created, as in the posters in

ABATTEZ-LE PAR VOTRE TRAVAIL

58.

which various people make their appeal by pointing at us with their finger.

Most of these locally made posters have quite a bit of text in the language of the particular group that they are addressing. In constrast, the War Posters Service (see Halliday, 1992), set up around 1916 by the federal government, produced poster series for national fund-raising campaigns, food preservation, and so on, with identical illustrations and text systematically repeated in English and French.

All of these posters were lithographs produced by the largest printing companies of the time, most of which were based in Toronto, Montreal, and Hamilton. The locally produced posters usually bore the name of the printer, but no credit was given on posters for the national campaigns.

To my knowledge, the print runs varied enormously, ranging from several hundred up to fifty thousand for posters such as "Heros of St. Julian and Festubert" (thirty-five thousand in English and fifteen thousand in French).

Except for a very few dated posters, the dating problem is difficult to resolve. Certainly, allusion to events sometimes enables us to discern a period. The disappearance of a printer during the war, as when Stone Ltd. was absorbed into Rolph, Clark, Stone Ltd. in 1918, can in a few cases provide a clue. As a general rule, however, we do not know the precise date of issue for First World War posters.

The situation is very different with regard to Second World War posters. Although Canada was again caught short at the beginning of the war, this time the federal government moved quickly to centralize and control everything having to do with war information.

Difficulties arose from internal struggles, many political men proving to be very reluctant to move from information to propaganda; the opposition Conservatives feared that the Liberal government would appropriate these instruments for their ends. Experts warned that educated citizens such as Canadians would not be taken in by unsophisticated propaganda of the type used during the First World War; in any case, the strength of a democracy was motivation and the decision freely made by everyone to participate in collective effort. Some pundits remarked that if the federal government controlled and censored all information and manipulated public opinion, it would be no different from Nazi Germany, for it would be using Dr. Goebbels's methods.

On September 9, 1939, the government created the Bureau of Public Information within the Department of National Defence. In July, 1940, the Department of National War Services was created; at its head was James Garfield Gardiner, the minister of agriculture, who held the post until June 10, 1941. Joseph T. Thorson replaced him until September of 1942, when all information agencies were restructured.

The Bureau of Public Information's Poster Division, with Albert Cloutier as artistic director, published a number of posters he commissioned for the Food Information Committee, the National Salvage Office, the Department of Munitions and Supply, the Department of Labour, and others. To design the posters, Cloutier called on friends who were freelance graphic designers, such as Henri Eveleigh, artists he knew who were employed in various army corps, such as Eric Aldwinckle and Roger Couillard, or, most frequently, on large advertising agencies, mostly in Toronto, which would also be responsible for printing and sometimes for distribution.

As of September 9, 1942, the Bureau of Public Information came under the control of the Wartime Information Board. Starting in February, 1943, the director general of the Board was John Grierson, the commissioner of the National Film Board since October, 1939. Holding these two positions, Grierson was in charge of most government propaganda until his departure, in January, 1944. The Documents and Bulletins Division of the Bureau of Public Information became the Posters and Publications Design Section of the Wartime Information Board's Graphics Division. Harry Mayerovitch, whose work Grierson had noticed at an exhibition, was named art director of the Graphics Division (which also included a Photo Services Section, then a Display Section as of August, 1944), and he was succeeded by Geoffrey Bagley in the summer of 1944.

The Board was in charge of producing posters for major campaigns initiated by various government departments and agencies, and the posters were credited to them. About sixty-five posters were created, the most remarkable being the twenty-two for the "Canada Carries On" films and the fourteen for

59.

60.

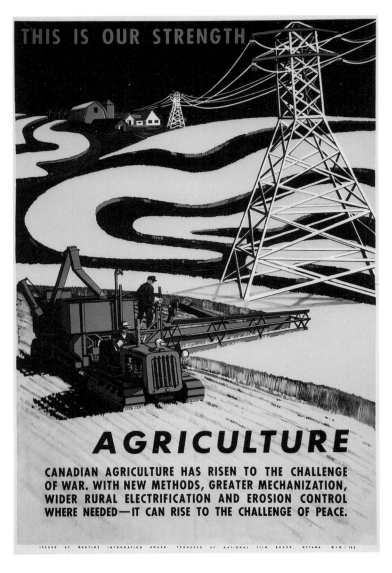

61.

the "World in Action" series, many of which were signed by Mayerovitch using the pseudonym "Mayo."

Both before and after the restructuring, however, many posters were made outside of this central control. Various processes led to poster production. Sometimes a local initiative by an individual (graphic artists, like Hubert Rogers, offered their services) or a company led to production of a poster. The largest airplane manufacturers bore the cost of printing some posters, as did the T. Eaton Co. Ltd., a few banks, and the Canadian Pacific Railway Co. Sometimes they were the work of official war artists, notably those for the air force, at the request of a government department or agency. Sometimes, though rarely, posters were printed as the result of a competition, such as Alfred Casson's for the 1941 war loans.

Greater centralization of production and a desire for homogeneity were behind the systematic printing of almost all posters in both languages. The result was sometimes curious and occasionally undesirable, as in the case of a poster portraying injured men: the caption on the French version read "It's your turn" (to be like them ?) a misinterpretation of the caption on the English version, "It's your move."

Much of the look and text of these posters, most of them made to order, was standardized in advance. The artist's only latitude was interpretation, for which he earned between $50 and $250, paid, in many cases, in bonds.

The posters, often printed in very large quantities (the six posters for the fourth victory-bond issue, in April, 1943, had print runs of 75,000 each), were printed using offset lithography. Some posters, however, were silkscreened, including those for the National Film Board's "Canada Carries On" and "The World in Action" series.

Unlike those made during the First World War, the posters for the Second World War never bore the name of the printer. The National Film Board's silkscreened posters were probably printed at General Advertising, in Lachine. For the others, it's difficult to know. However, one could posit, from the artists' names appearing on some of them, that they were produced as part of contracts awarded to the companies that were employing the particular artists, mainly large Toronto agencies.

On the other hand, it is possible to date quite accurately the many posters that bear a long credit line mentioning the Bureau of Public Information, sometimes even that of the minister responsible, or the National Film Board. Some newspaper articles and documents dealing with the loan issues, as well as a study by Young and Rubicam, have also enabled me to date some of the posters presented herein.

Distribution of the posters also changed: after the Bureau of Public Information was set up, it became systematic. In 1943, when Grierson took over the entire organization, the number of distribution points rose from five thousand to twenty-three thousand, including hotels, restaurants, taverns, boutiques, hairdressing salons and beauty parlours, and train stations. In November, 1943, alone, 157,660 posters were distributed, including more than thirty thousand of "I was a victim of careless talk" (see Mayerovitch in the colour plates) and more than 28,000 of the "Men of Valor" series (by Hubert Rogers).

Throughout the war, the effectiveness of the posters was questioned. Charles Vining, who was briefly the first chairman of the Bureau of Public Information, from September of 1942 to the end of January, 1943, felt that "the daily news clearly has a greater impact on morale than do pamphlets, notices, and posters" (Young, 1978, p. 42). Thus, in 1942–43, the Commission allocated only 6.4% out of a budget of a little more than a million dollars to poster production. In June, 1943, Grierson, in a confidential memorandum, presented an overview of the situation concerning all forms of propaganda. According to this document, radio and the newspapers were favourites among the public, far ahead of films and magazines, which were followed by posters and pamphlets. On the other hand, he noted that posters were viewed much more favourably in Quebec and British Columbia, especially by white-collar workers in large cities.

The type of posters produced was also criticized. At the end of 1942, a debate took place in the newspapers. Cloutier defended the Bureau of Public Information and its production by saying that he paid well and had tried to get good artists to design posters, but the results had been disappointing. Exhibitions of Soviet war posters, like that held in the central hall of Windsor Station in Montreal in late 1942 and early

62.

1943, seem to have stimulated these criticisms, for the Canadian posters paled greatly in comparison.

The publicity around the study by the Toronto agency Young and Rubicam, undertaken in the spring of 1942 and presented that autumn, also stimulated a debate on the very nature of graphic design. According to this study, the most effective posters were the purely emotional ones, appealing to sentiment through realistic images with photographic details, accessible to millions of middle-class citizens. It rejected abstract and symbolic illustrations and considered humour not very attractive. This study was itself criticized and questioned by the Bureau's consultants, but most Canadian war posters in fact followed the principles it laid out.

63.

It is not easy to gather biographical information on poster artists, and even less so on those who worked in Canada. Most of the many books on posters deal with their quality and meaning, rather than the artists who designed them and the techniques used to produce them.

As for the artists who created posters during the two world wars, only those who had other recognized artistic production have sometimes been listed in directories of artists. In fact, many of the best war posters were the work of anonymous graphic designers (or "commercial artists," the more derogatory title they are often assigned) in the employ of printers or advertising agencies. Below is the information I have been able to gather; in many cases, however, the enigma is almost complete.

ADAMS, John
No information on this artist could be found..

ADAMSON, Caporal
While serving in Holland, he took part in a poster competition for the eighth loan issue and won first prize among the entries sent from overseas.

ALDWINCKLE, Eric
Born in Oxford, England, January 22, 1909.
Soon after he arrived in Canada, in the early 1920s, his father died and he had to take care of his family. A self-taught artist, he was working as a freelance graphic designer in Toronto in 1928. He was a member of the Canadian Society of Graphic Arts and became a member of the Ontario Society of Artists in 1936, when he began teaching at the Ontario College of Art. He signed up for the Royal Canadian Air Force in 1942 and was an official war artist from 1943 to 1945. He produced many war posters inspired by the Soviet school; in 1944, he served in France and Belgium. When he came home, in 1945, he was appointed vice-president of the Ontario College of Art; in 1946, he was named director of the New School of Design.

64.

65.

Over the years, he held various positions at the university and in Toronto art circles.

He died on January 13, 1980.

ARBUCKLE, George Franklin

Born in Toronto, Ontario, February 17, 1909.

After studying at the Ontario College of Art, notably under J.E.H. MacDonald, he made his living selling his paintings and giving courses in art schools. He worked as a graphic designer for Bomac Federal Ltd. in Ottawa and Montreal until 1944, then returned to painting. He produced a number of magazine covers for Maclean's, as well as murals and tapestries. In the 1960s, he taught at the Ontario College of Art and was president of the Royal Canadian Academy.

He died around 1988.

BOOK, W.

No information could be found on this artist, although he did produce a poster for the Canadian Pacific Railway Co. (see Choko and Jones, 1988).

CASSON, Alfred Joseph

Born in Toronto, Ontario, May 17, 1898.

After studying at the Ryerson School, he took courses at the Hamilton Technical School. He worked as an apprentice at the Laidlaw Lithography Company in Hamilton. In 1916, he followed his parents to Toronto, where he worked and took night courses at the Ontario College of Art. In 1919, he met Franklin Carmichael, for whom he worked as an assistant graphic designer at Rous and Mann Ltd. After launching a freelance career in 1926, when he became a member of the Group of Seven, replacing Franz Johnston, he became art director and vice-president of Sampson-Matthews Ltd., where he remained for almost twenty years.

In 1941, the poster he created for victory bonds was selected from almost a hundred designs and repeatedly reproduced in large numbers.

He became vice-president of the Royal Canadian Academy in 1945, and was the Academy's president from 1948 to 1952.

In 1959 and throughout the 1960s, he exhibited his paintings.

He died on February 19, 1992.

CLOUTIER, Albert Edward

Born of Canadian parents in Leominster, Massachusetts, 1902.

He arrived in Canada in 1903 and, encouraged by his parents, started art courses very young at the Monument National in Montreal, then with A.Y. Jackson and Edwin Holgate. Self-taught, he worked as a graphic artist for many years. Among others, he designed the posters for the Liberal Party of Quebec's 1935 campaign. He became artistic director of the Bureau of Public Information, then was an official war artist for the Royal Canadian Air Force from 1943 to 1946.

He produced many murals, including one for the Canada Pavilion at the New York World's Fair in 1939.

He died in 1965.

COUILLARD, Roger
Born in Montreal, Quebec, March 21, 1910

After finishing grade 10, Couillard attended the Fine Arts School in Montreal for one year. He then decided to leave school to begin a commercial practice and worked as a church and theatre decorator at Salette et Fils for two years. In 1932, he became a decorator for the Matou Botté, a popular cabaret on St. Denis Street. When Nesbitt-Thomson purchased the Ogilvy department stores, Couillard became the decorator for the outlet on St. Catherine Street, increasing his involvement in commercial art. He travelled to New York and Chicago to compare styles and window-display designs. In 1935, the Institute of Foreign Travel organized a poster competition on the theme "See Europe Next." Couillard's poster was among those chosen to be exhibited in the Ogilvy store. In 1937, he opened his own graphic-design studio, on St. Catherine Street, in the Drummond Building. In order to get commissions from both French- and English-language clients, he used the name Studio Coutrey. He started to create his own poster designs, which he offered to a variety of companies. Before the end of the year, Couillard had reworked his poster for Europe, which became "See Europe Next by Empress of Britain." John Murray Gibbon, the general advertising agent for the Canadian Pacific Railway Co., was impressed by Couillard's work, and the poster was immediately printed for distribution

The following year, Couillard produced another poster for CPR, "Alaska." But it was Canadian National Railways that became his main client, ordering a dozen posters. During this period, Couillard also designed posters for the city of Montreal and the province of Quebec. In 1943, he joined the Royal Canadian Air Force. He was granted leave periodically to work for the Ardiel Advertising Agency, a Toronto firm that had the contract with the War Department to design publicity campaigns for war bonds. Couillard created six posters, for which he received one hundred dollars each (in war bonds). In 1945, he left he army and returned to his commercial-art practice in Montreal. In 1947, he moved his studio to Sainte-Adèle, Quebec. Again, most of his commissions were done for a competitor of CPR, Canadian Steamship Lines, for which he designed a series of posters and pamphlets in 1952. However, he

66.

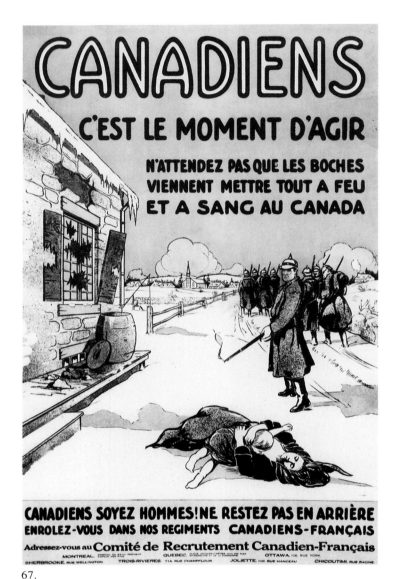

CANADIENS
C'EST LE MOMENT D'AGIR
N'ATTENDEZ PAS QUE LES BOCHES VIENNENT METTRE TOUT A FEU ET A SANG AU CANADA

CANADIENS SOYEZ HOMMES! NE RESTEZ PAS EN ARRIÈRE
ENROLEZ-VOUS DANS NOS REGIMENTS CANADIENS-FRANÇAIS
Adressez-vous au Comité de Recrutement Canadien-Français

67.

contributed to the CPR display in the Railway pavilion at the Canadian National Exhibition in Toronto in 1948 and was involved in a number of CPR publicity campaigns, creating the "White Empress to Europe" poster, among others. In the mid-1950s, Couillard painted large maps for use in railway passenger coaches. Another client of Couillard's was Herdt and Charton Inc., a Montreal perfume and alcohol importer. Most of his production work was done by General Advertising, the Hirsch family's printing company located in Lachine, Quebec. In 1952, he won the poster competition that celebrated the anniversary of Newfoundland's entry into Confederation three years earlier. With the expansion of colour photography and the drop in the market for graphic design, Couillard got involved in the hotel business. In 1957, he became president of the Montclair Hotel in Sainte-Adèle. In 1964, he moved to the Chantecler Hotel, where he was named vice-president and general manager. In 1966, he became inspector of hotels for the Quebec department of tourism, where he stayed until he retired, in 1975

He lives in Sainte-Adèle, Quebec

DAVID, Charles
This was probably the architect Charles David, born in Montreal on April 5, 1890.

Following his architectural studies at the Montreal Polytechnical School and Pennsylvania State University, he enlisted in 1914 and served until 1918 as a lieutenant in the Canadian Engineers. Returning to civilian life, he worked mainly in Montreal. From 1939 to 1945, David directed Wartime Housing Ltd. He became president of the Province of Quebec Association of Architects in 1948 and of the Royal Architecture Institute of Canada.

He died in 1962.

EVELEIGH, Henri
Born in Shanghai, China, to English parents, July 26, 1909.

Returning to England with his parents, he studied at the Slade School of Fine Arts at the University of London, where he won first prize for posters for Lissue Co. He produced other posters during the 1930s to make a living, but he was already becoming known for his paintings. When he emigrated to Canada, in 1938, he lived in Montreal, where he became friends with Alfred Cloutier and Charles Fainmel, who got him into Woodward Press as an apprentice. Starting in 1939, he worked as a freelance graphic designer. It was Cloutier, now art director of the Bureau of Public Information, who gave him the commission for the "Let's Go Canada" poster. He produced some other posters for the war effort, including a series for the Royal Bank. In 1947, he won first prize in an international poster competition for the United Nations and his poster was seen around the world. He also won first prize in the Canadian awards in 1948. After he was named director of the new department of advertising graphic design at the Montreal's School of Fine Art in 1947, he continued to work as a graphic designer, first on his own, then with Carl Dair, and finally in the Cossman, Eveleigh, Dair advertising agency. From 1969 to 1971, he was the first director of the graphic-design module at *Université du Québec à Montréal*, where he taught until 1981. Following his retirement, he turned to painting. He lives in Rosemère, Quebec

FAINMEL, Charles

According to his "adopted son," Ivan Fainmel, the son from a first marriage of the woman who became Charles Fainmel's wife in 1941, Marguerite Paquette, Fainmel was born in Poland in 1903 (although the National Directory gives the date as 1904) and arrived in Canada when he was a few months old. His father was a lithographic printer.

Charles Fainmel studied sculpture at Montreal's Monument National, then left for Paris in the late 1920s or early 1930s, where he was an apprentice in graphic design under Cassandre (for Adolphe Mouron). In 1933, he returned to Montreal with Marguerite Paquette, and they worked together as freelance graphic designers. Their business went under during the Depression and he went to work at Woodward Press in 1937–38, where he was employed until the late 1950s.

He died around 1971.

FINLEY, Frederick James

Born in Newcastle, Australia, in 1894.

He began drawing during First World War, then studied at the Sydney Art School, Académie Julian in Paris, and the Bavarian Academy. In 1925, he came to Canada, where he worked as a graphic designer in Toronto, first at Brigdens Ltd., from 1927 to 1939, then at Baker-Ashdown Ltd., from 1941 to 1945. He took courses at the Ontario College of Art and taught there after the war. He became director of the advertising and graphic design department in 1946, and director of the college in 1960.

He died in 1968.

GAGNON, M.

This could be Maurice Gagnon, born August 13, 1912, in Winnipeg, Manitoba.

After studying in Europe, he obtained a bachelor's degree at *Université Laval*. He worked in Montreal as a freelance journalist and in advertising. In 1939, he signed up in the Royal Canadian Navy. After the war, he wrote a number of short novels and children's stories.

68.

69.

70.

GIBSON, Malcolm

Although he certainly produced one of the best series of Canadian posters for First World War, Gibson remains completely unknown, probably because he spent his career as a "commercial artist." Only Colgate alludes to his life, mentioning that he often went to the Graphic Arts Club in Toronto with Joseph Ernest Sampson and Frank Carmichael.

Gibson was first listed in the Toronto city directory in 1913 as a lithographer. From 1914 to 1916, he was a graphic designer at Stone Ltd.; in 1919 he worked at Color Craft Ltd., then at Sampson. Starting in 1921, he seems to have been working as an artist, probably freelance. In 1941, he was again listed as a lithographer, this time for Offset Photo-Composed Plate Co. Ltd., and was living in Richvale. No Second World War posters that he may have designed were identified. In 1945, he was working as an artist at Ashton Potter, where he remained until 1953, when he probably died.

HARRIS, Ted

No information was found for this graphic designer, who was working during Second World War.

HARRISON, Allan

Born in Montreal, Quebec, December 27, 1911.

He studied at the School of Fine Arts in 1929 and 1930, then went to London, where he lived from 1933 to 1935 and began to design posters, notably for the Marks and Spencer stores. He met Raoul Bonin, a graphic artist from Montreal, in Paris in 1938. When he returned to Montreal, he became art director at J. Walter Thompson Co. Ltd., a position he held from 1940 to 1946, when he also taught advertising graphic design at the Art Association of Montreal (which became the Montreal Museum of Fine Arts). Like many artists at the time, Harrison was close to the Communist Party and designed the 1944 election poster for Fred Rose, the only federal communist member of parliament ever elected in Canada (Cartier riding in Montreal). Harrison left to work as an art director in Rio de Janeiro in 1946 and 1947, then in New York in the 1950s. When he returned to Montreal, he designed a number of remarkable posters for the Medical Arts Pharmacy and, later, posters for the fund-raising campaign for *Place des Arts*. During this time, he kept painting, and was much better known as an artist.

He died in Montreal on March 4, 1988.

HENDERSON, E.

No information could be found on this graphic designer, who was extremely active during First World War at Howell Litho. in Hamilton, Ontario.

HIDER, Arthur H.
Born in 1870.

His career as an artist began in 1889 at Grant Litho. Co. in Toronto. In 1890, he was working at Barclay, Clark and Co.; in 1893 he was at C.E. Preston and Co. Between 1894 and 1908, he was a lithographer, then from 1908 to 1910 he was a graphic designer, at Toronto Litho. Co. During this time he produced a number of military illustrations, including a series in collaboration with John David Kelly, in 1906, printed by Globe Printing Co. After working as a freelance graphic artist until 1923, he went in-house at Rolph, Clark, Stone Ltd., where he remained until he died, in 1952.

KEELOR, Arthur
Born in 1890.

He began working as an artist at Hough Litho. Co., in Toronto, in 1910, where he worked until 1916, when he went freelance. From 1921 to 1942, he was a graphic designer at Rous and Mann Ltd., then a freelance designer again from 1945 to 1949. Curiously, he does not seem to have designed any posters during Second World War. He probably moved away from Toronto or died in 1949 or 1950.

LEONARD, Jac
This may have been Jack de Coudres Léonard, an American architect, illustrator, and graphic designer, born in 1903.

MACDONALD, James Edward Hervey
Born in Durham, England, in 1873, to a Canadian father.

His family returned to Canada in 1887 and set up house in Hamilton, Ontario, where he took night courses at the Hamilton Art School, under John Preland and Arthur Hening. Around 1890, the family moved to Toronto, where he became an apprentice at the Toronto Lithography Co. In 1893, he took more courses at the Central Ontario School of Art and Design. In 1895, he took a job as a graphic designer at Grip Ltd. He was a member of the Toronto Art Students League as of about 1902. He went to London in 1903, where he worked at Carlton Studios until 1907. When he returned to Toronto with his wife and son, he went to work again at Grip Ltd. He travelled and painted with various friends, many of whom he met at Grip Ltd., who would form the Group of Seven. At the end of 1917, exhausted, worried, and depressed by the accidental death of his friend Tom Thompson, MacDonald had a heart attack. When he recovered, he travelled again to paint the northern Ontario forest. Around 1920, he became a professor of decorative art and graphic design at the Ontario College of Art. He travelled and painted some more, then became director of

71.

72.

73.

the Ontario College of Art in 1928, and its principal in 1929.

He had another heart attack in the winter of 1930. After he returned from his convalescence in Barbados, he died in his office on November 26, 1932, of yet another heart attack.

McLAREN, Alex L.

Born in Lisbon, Portugal, in 1892, to Scottish parents.

His father died in 1900 and he returned with his mother to Scotland, where he studied at the Dundee School of Art. He arrived in Montreal in 1911, where his brother was living, and worked as an estimator and cashier. During this time, he studied painting at the School of Fine Art under Edmond Dyonnet. From 1934 to 1941, he worked as a freelance graphic designer; in 1943 he, L. Banks, and Roy E. Dyer created the Crescent Art Group, within which he worked until 1957. In 1958, he was still in Montreal working as a freelance graphic designer.

He left Montreal or died in 1959.

MAYEROVITCH, Harry

Born in Montreal, Quebec, April 16, 1910, to parents of Romanian origin.

He obtained a bachelor's degree in fine arts, then one in architecture, at McGill University in 1933. In 1934, he became a member of the Province of Quebec Association of Architects and began to practice in Montreal. He also began to paint and travelled in Mexico, where he was influenced by the painters Diego Rivera and Jose Clemente Orozco. John Grierson, who had seen one of his paintings at an exhibition, offered him the position of art director of the Graphic Arts Division of the Bureau of Public Information, even though, like many other artists of the time, he had ties to the Communist Party. His brother, David Mayerovitch, already worked at the National Film Board. Mayerovitch accepted, and worked in Ottawa from 1942 to 1944, signing a number of remarkable posters for propaganda films and various campaigns with the pseudonym "Mayo." He received the first and third prizes for Canadian war posters in 1944. At the same time, he did political caricatures for the newspapers The Standard and Le Jour. After the war, he worked as an architect in Montreal, where he was also active on various urban-development committees. A member of the Montreal Citizens' Committee, he was vice-president of the group in 1965. He worked as a consultant for the cities of Montreal, Westmount, and Jerusalem and taught architecture at Université Laval and McGill University. He drew and painted all through his career, and had a number of exhibitions, including one at the National Arts Centre in Ottawa, in 1981. Mayerovitch also had published a book of his poems, a book of his political caricatures, and a book he wrote on urban development. He lives in Westmount, Quebec, where he paints and works as an architectural consultant.

MORRIS

A certain G.R. Morris produced many posters very similar to the style in the "Be Discreet" series (see colour plates), but he worked in England. (See Darracott and Loftus, 1972.)

NICHOL

This could be Peter Nichol, born around 1912 in Slavgorod, Siberia, and an immigrant to western Canada as a child.

He lived and worked in Hamilton until 1955. Then he moved to Deep River, Ontario, where he was a machinist at the Chalk River Nuclear Laboratories. All this time, he was interested in art, notably wood sculpture.

NOBBS, Percy Erskine

Born in Haddington, Scotland, August 11, 1875.

After spending his childhood at St. Petersburg, he entered Edinburgh Collegiate School in 1887. In 1896, he obtained a master's degree in architecture and urban development, and worked in Edinburgh at Robert Lorimer. He took courses at the Edinburgh School of Art, R. Anderson Applied Arts, and Heriot Watt College. When he finished his apprenticeship, in 1900, he became a member of the Royal Institute of British Architects. After travelling in Italy, Nobbs moved to London in 1901, where he worked at the London County Council. In June, 1903, he met William Peterson, the principal of McGill University, who offered him the MacDonald Chair in the Faculty of Architecture, which he accepted. He executed a number of contracts in and around Montreal. In 1909, he was a founder of the Montreal City Improvement League. In 1912, he produced the landscaping plan for the University of Alberta in Edmonton. He enlisted in 1915 and served in France, rising to the rank of major by the end of the war. During this time, he painted rural scenes, and he continued to paint throughout his life.

In 1924, he was president of the Province of Quebec Association of Architects, and in 1928 he headed the Town Planning Institute of Canada. He was a consultant for the city of Montreal's Urban Planning Department, created in 1941.

He died in Montreal on November 5, 1964.

ODELL, Gordon K.

From 1921 to 1927, he was listed in the Montreal Lovell directory as a freelance artist . He joined (or founded) Canadian Associated Artists in 1928, becoming its president and marketing director in 1929. From 1936 to 1946, he owned this company. He then was art director at

74.

75.

76.

Rolph, Clark, Stone Ltd. in Montreal from 1947 to 1950. Between 1950 and 1953, he was sales director.

He disappeared from the Montreal directory in 1954.

PATTERSON, C.J.

This may be John Patterson, an artist at Grip Ltd. in Toronto in 1916, then a freelance graphic designer in 1921.

It is also possible that the poster was designed by an Englishman named C.J. Patterson, printed in England, and then copied in Canada. (In fact, one version of this poster is marked David Allen and Sons Ltd., The Parliamentary Recruiting Committee, London.)

ROGERS, Hubert

Born in Prince Edward Island, 1898.

He served in the Royal Canadian Artillery during the First World War. After art training in Toronto and Boston, he worked as an illustrator in 1925 in New York for a number of newspapers and publishers. He designed some fifty covers for Adventure, and in 1939 he designed covers for Astounding Science. He offered his services to Ottawa in 1940; in 1942, he designed the series of five "Men of Valor" posters, then "Attack on All Fronts," and finally "Fight for Tomorrow," which was never printed (see Dorais, 1991). After the war ended, he returned to the United States, where he continued his career as illustrator and painter. By the mid-1960s, he was living in Brattleboro, Vermont, and Manotick, Ontario.

He died in 1982.

SAMPSON, Joseph Ernest

Born in Liverpool, England, July 11, 1887, he emigrated to Canada.

A member of the Toronto Graphic Arts Club at the same time as Malcolm Gibson and Frank Carmichael, he was a graphic designer at Stone Ltd. in 1914, where he stayed until 1919. During this time, he designed a number of war posters. From 1919 to 1922, Sampson was vice-president of Color Craft Ltd., becoming president in 1923. He was then president of Sampson-Matthews Ltd. from 1924 to 1941. He designed a few more war posters during the Second World War.

He died on October 29, 1946, in York Mills, Ontario.

STAPLETON, Archibald Bruce

Born in Stratford, Ontario, on July 19, 1910.

After starting as a salesman at R.G. McLean in Toronto around 1937, he became an artist for this company in 1939, also working for Rolph, Clark, Stone Ltd. at the same time. He worked at the latter company as a graphic designer from 1940 to 1948. He then went to Brigdens Ltd., where he remained from 1949 to 1953. In 1954, he became art director at E.S. and A. Robinson Ltd.

STEWART, Clair C.
Born on May 20, 1910, in Kenton, Manitoba.
He worked as a graphic designer for McLaren and McCaul Ltd. in Toronto from 1938 to 1943, then became art director at Rolph, Clark, Stone Ltd., where he remained until 1960. He then was co-founder of Stewart and Morrison Ltd., which he directed until the mid-1980s.

SURREY, Philip Henry Howard
Born on October 10, 1910, in Calgary, Alberta.
He studied at the Winnipeg School of Art under Lemoine Fitzgerald in 1926–27, then at the Vancouver School of Art between 1930 and 1932. During this time, he worked as a graphic designer, first at Brigdens of Winnipeg Ltd., then at Cleland-Kent Engraving in Vancouver. He studied at the Art Students League in New York from 1936 to 1937, under Alexander Abels.
From 1937 to 1964, he was photo editor then art editor of Weekend Magazine at the Montreal Star, at the same time pursuing a career as a painter.
He died in Montreal on April 23, 1990.

TABER, Russel A.J.
He was an artist at Brigdens Ltd. in Toronto in 1936, then set up his own company, TDF Advertising Ltd., in 1948 (with W.H. Dulmage and M.F. Feheley). He became president of the firm in 1952.

TREVOR, Leslie J.
He was an artist at Rous and Mann Ltd. in Toronto from 1928 to 1945. After the war, he became art director at the firm.

WHITE, Ron
No information was found for this graphic designer, who was very active during the Second World War.

WILCOX, Charles Richard
He lived in Halifax up to the end of the 1920s, when he moved to Toronto. In 1937 and 1938, he was a freelance graphic designer, then from 1939 to 1946 he worked as an artist at E.S. and A. Robinson Ltd. in Toronto. From 1948 to 1951, he was an artist at Planned Sales Ltd., when he seems to have left Toronto.
He probably died in 1970.

77.

78.

COLOUR ILLUSTRATIONS

For the Second World War, no format is indicated for posters, as most of them were printed in the standard 61x 90 cm format, though some were also printed as small posters, window posters, and so on.

I
Anonymous, c. 1917–18
Lithograph, 102 x 143
(N.A.C. 977843)

Buy Your Victory Bonds

D-1

II
A. ? R., c. 1915
Lithograph, 69 x 104
Consolidated Lithographing and Mfg. Co. Ltd.,
Montreal
(The Carson Coll.)

CANADIENS FRANCAIS

VENEZ AVEC NOUS DANS LE
150 ième BATAILLON C.M.R
AIDER A LA VICTOIRE DU COQ GAULOIS SUR
L'AIGLE PRUSSIEN

Lt. Col. H. Barré
Chev de la legion d'honneur

Arsenal du 65 ième Ave des Pins
Salle d'exercice Rue Craig

III
Anonymous, c. 1917
Lithograph, 61 x 92
(The Carson Coll.)

Doing My Bit
FOUR YEARS

DO YOURS
BUY
Victory Bonds

W.P. 4.

IV
Anonymous, c. 1915
Lithograph, 69 x 105
Montreal Litho. Co. Ltd.
(McGill University)

V
Anonymous, c. 1915
Lithograph, 69 x 104
The Mortimer Co. Ltd., Ottawa, Montreal
(The Carson Coll.)

LE 178 IEME BATAILLON CANADIEN-FRANÇAIS
DES CANTONS DE L'EST
"LES PURS CANAYENS"

FAIS CE QUE DOIS ADVIENNE QUE POURRA

MONTRONS QUE NOUS SOMMES DE RACE FIÈRE ET LOYALE.

LE 178 IEME BATAILLON DES CANTONS DE L'EST SERA COMMANDÉ PAR LE LIEUTENANT-COLONEL DE LA BRUÈRE GIROUARD ET PAR AU MOINS CINQ OFFICIERS DE L'HÉROIQUE 22 IEME QUI FAIT AU FRONT L'HONNEUR ET L'ORGUEIL DES CANADIENS-FRANÇAIS

VI
Anonymous, c. 1915
Lithograph, 70 x 105
Montreal Litho. Co. Ltd.
(McGill University)

WE GO NEXT!

OVERSEAS IRISH·CANADIAN·RANGERS
199
QUIS SEPARABIT

BE ONE OF THE
IRISH CANADIAN RANGERS
OVERSEAS BATTALION
Under Lt. Col. H. J. TRIHEY.
Headquarters · 91 Stanley St., Montreal.

VII
Anonymous, c. 1915
Lithograph, 70 x 106
The Mortimer Co. Ltd., Ottawa, Montreal
(N.A.C. C-95378)

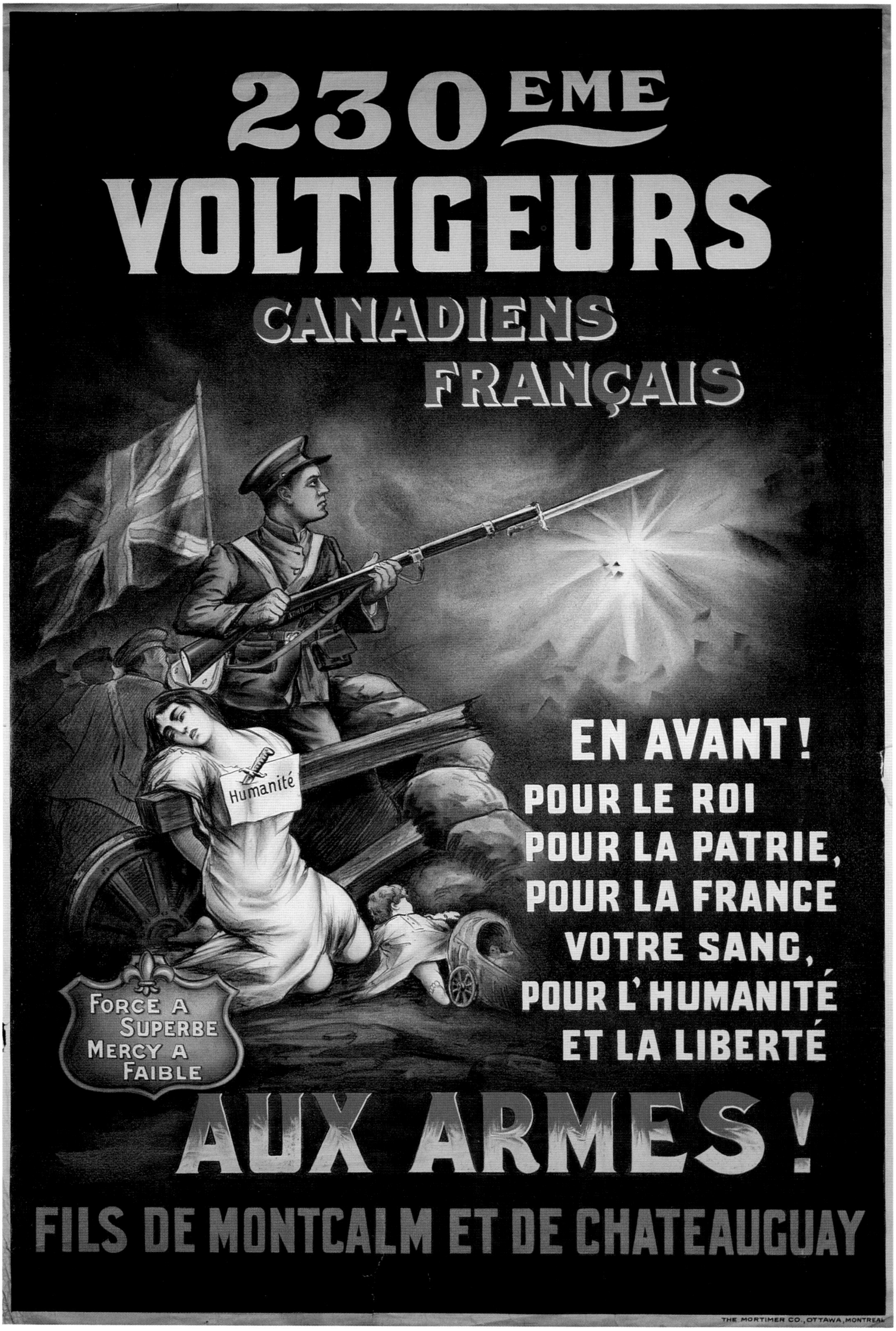
230EME
VOLTIGEURS
CANADIENS
FRANÇAIS
Humanité
EN AVANT!
POUR LE ROI
POUR LA PATRIE,
POUR LA FRANCE
VOTRE SANG,
POUR L'HUMANITÉ
ET LA LIBERTÉ
FORCE A SUPERBE MERCY A FAIBLE
AUX ARMES!
FILS DE MONTCALM ET DE CHATEAUGUAY
THE MORTIMER CO., OTTAWA, MONTREAL

VIII
Anonymous, c. 1915
Lithograph, 63 x 97
Stone Ltd.
(N.A.C. C-29484)

Your Chums are Fighting

Why aren't YOU?

No. 2   Central Recruiting Committee, No. 2 Military Division, Toronto

Stone Lito

IX
P.E. Nobbs, c. 1915
Lithograph, 69 x 105
J.J. Gibbons Ltd., Montreal, Toronto
(The Carson Coll.)

X
W. TOPPLE and O.M. HOUSE, c. 1915
Lithograph, 82 x 110
(N.A.C. C-109764)

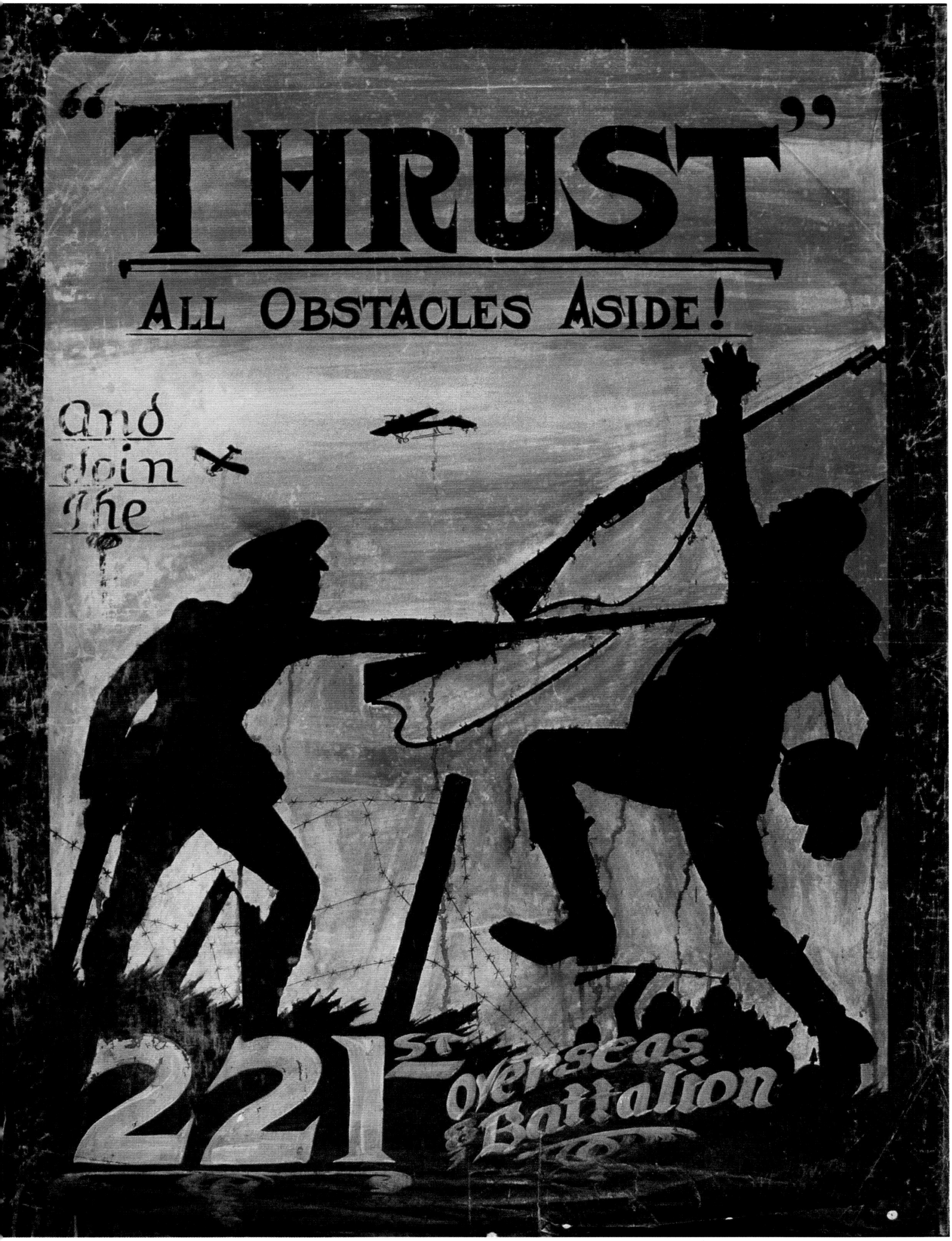
"THRUST"
ALL OBSTACLES ASIDE!
And Join The
221st Overseas Battalion

XI
Anonymous, c. 1915
Lithograph, 70 x 107
The Mortimer Co. Ltd., Ottawa, Montreal

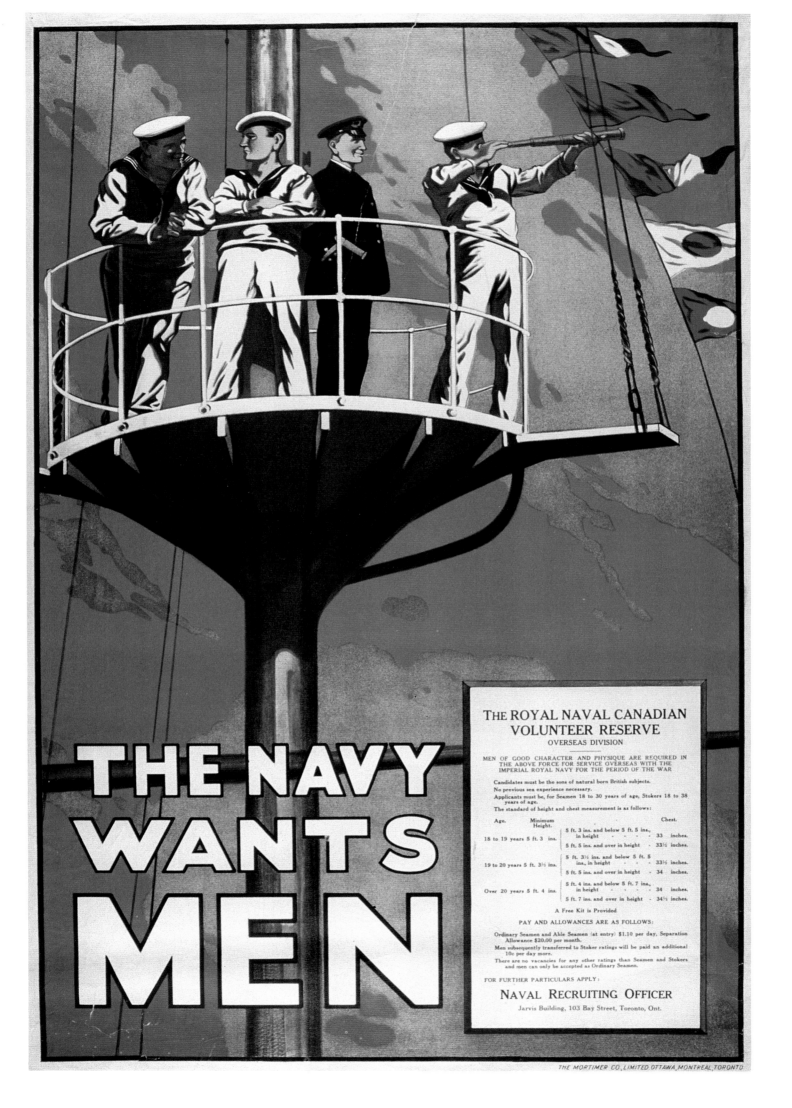

THE NAVY
WANTS
MEN

THE ROYAL NAVAL CANADIAN VOLUNTEER RESERVE
OVERSEAS DIVISION

MEN OF GOOD CHARACTER AND PHYSIQUE ARE REQUIRED IN THE ABOVE FORCE FOR SERVICE OVERSEAS WITH THE IMPERIAL ROYAL NAVY FOR THE PERIOD OF THE WAR

Candidates must be the sons of natural born British subjects.

No previous sea experience necessary.

Applicants must be, for Seamen 18 to 30 years of age, Stokers 18 to 38 years of age.

The standard of height and chest measurement is as follows:

Age.	Minimum Height.		Chest.
18 to 19 years	5 ft. 3 ins.	5 ft. 3 ins. and below 5 ft. 5 ins., in height	33 inches.
		5 ft. 5 ins. and over in height	33½ inches.
19 to 20 years	5 ft. 3½ ins.	5 ft. 3½ ins. and below 5 ft. 5 ins., in height	33½ inches.
		5 ft. 5 ins. and over in height	34 inches.
Over 20 years	5 ft. 4 ins.	5 ft. 4 ins. and below 5 ft. 7 ins., in height	34 inches.
		5 ft. 7 ins. and over in height	34½ inches.

A Free Kit is Provided

PAY AND ALLOWANCES ARE AS FOLLOWS:

Ordinary Seamen and Able Seamen (at entry) $1.10 per day, Separation Allowance $20.00 per month.

Men subsequently transferred to Stoker ratings will be paid an additional 10c per day more.

There are no vacancies for any other ratings than Seamen and Stokers and men can only be accepted as Ordinary Seamen.

FOR FURTHER PARTICULARS APPLY:

NAVAL RECRUITING OFFICER

Jarvis Building, 103 Bay Street, Toronto, Ont.

XII
Anonymous, 1918
Lithograph, 69 x 105
(The Carson Coll.)

ILS VAINCRONT
si vous souscrivez
à L'EMPRUNT
DE LA
VICTOIRE
1918

W. P. Nº 8.

XIII
Anonymous, 1918
Lithograph, 45 x 61
(The Carson Coll.)

KEEP ALL CANADIANS BUSY

BUY 1918 VICTORY BONDS

WP 11

XIV
J.E. SAMPSON, 1914–18
Lithograph, 60 x 90
(N.A.C. C-99708)

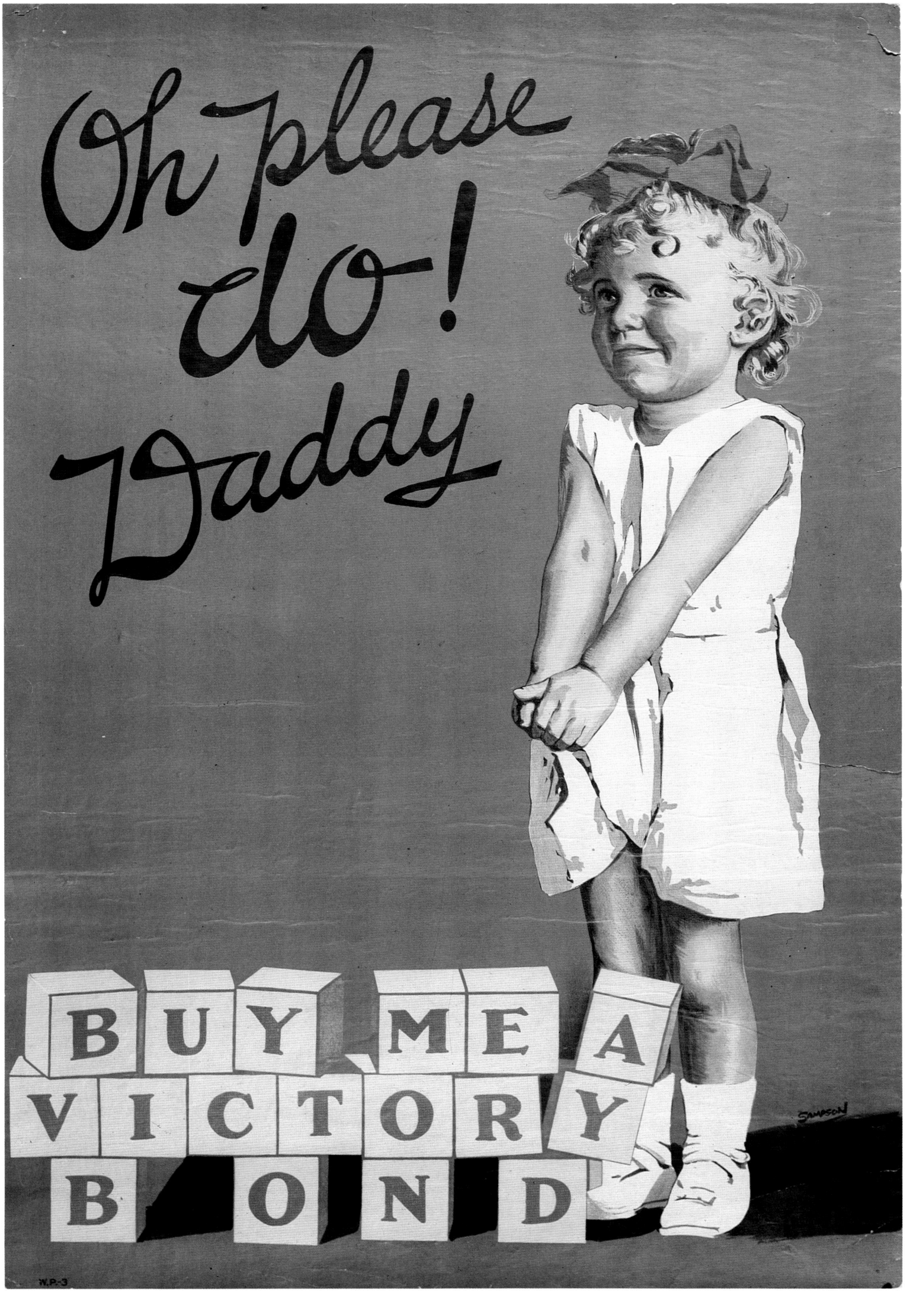
Oh please do! Daddy
BUY ME A
VICTORY
BOND
SAMPSON
W.P.-3

XV
F.L. NICOLET, 1914–18
Lithograph, 89 x 61
(M.G. NMC-722146)
Photograph: William Kent

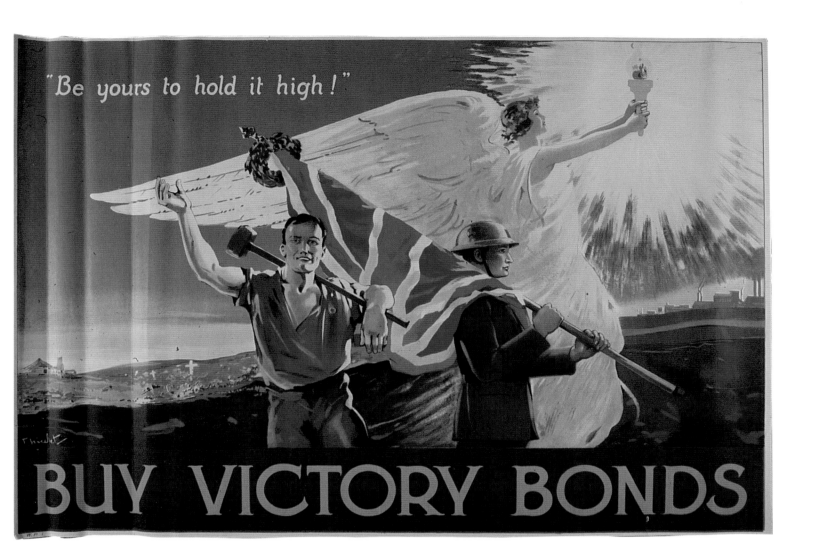

XVI
Anonymous, 1914–18
Lithograph, 44 x 60
(N.A.C.)

XVII
Arthur KEELOR, 1914–18
Lithograph, 61 x 91
(N.A.C. C-97753)

OUR EXPORT TRADE IS VITAL
BUY VICTORY BONDS

XVIII
Arthur KEELOR, 1914–18
Lithograph, 61 x 91
(N.A.C. C-119446)

XIX
Malcolm GIBSON, 1914–18
Lithograph, 61 x 92
(The Carson Coll.)

RIEN À
FAIRE —
sans
L'EMPRUNT DE LA VICTOIRE

MALCOLM
GIBSON

W.P. 4.

XX
Malcolm GIBSON, 1914–18
Lithograph, 61 x 90
(The Carson Coll.)

XXI
Anonymous, 1916
Lithograph, 69 x 101
Howell Litho. Ltd., Hamilton
(N.A.C. C-9870)

XXII
E. HENDERSON, 1914–18
Lithograph, 46 x 62
Howell Litho. Ltd., Hamilton
(N.A.C. C-95278)

XXIII
M.?, c. 1918
Lithograph, 68 x 104
(McGill University)

CANADA'S WORK
FOR
WOUNDED
SOLDIERS

XXIV
J.E.H. MACDONALD, 1914
Lithograph
Rolph and Clark, Toronto
(Robert Stacey Coll.)

"CANADA AND
THE CALL
1914"

EXHIBITION of PICTURES
GIVEN BY CANADIAN ARTISTS
IN AID of the PATRIOTIC FUND

UNDER THE AUSPICES OF
THE ROYAL CANADIAN ACADEMY

DESIGNED BY J.E.H. MacDONALD A.R.C.A.

ROLPH AND CLARK, TORONTO

XXV
Henri EVELEIGH, 1941–42
Lithograph
(The Carson Coll.)

Let's Go... CANADA!

ISSUED BY THE DIRECTOR OF PUBLIC INFORMATION, UNDER THE AUTHORITY OF HON. J. T. THORSON, MINISTER OF NATIONAL WAR SERVICES, OTTAWA.   PRINTED IN CANADA — UE - 15

XXVI
Eric ALDWINCKLE
and A.E. CLOUTIER, 1941–42
Lithograph
(The Carson Coll.)

CANADA'S NEW ARMY

NEEDS

MEN LIKE YOU

ISSUED FOR THE DEPT. OF NATIONAL DEFENCE BY THE DIRECTOR OF PUBLIC INFORMATION, OTTAWA.

XXVII
M. GAGNON, 1941
Silkscreen, 61 x 92
(M.G. NMC-7510980)
Photograph: William Kent

FOR CANADA THE EMPIRE AND FREEDOM

DO YOUR PART
ENLIST NOW
IN

THE ROYAL RIFLES OF CANADA

CANADIAN ACTIVE SERVICE FORCE

1862

IN AMALGAMATION WITH
THE 7/11TH HUSSARS

1867

RECRUITING STATIONS
AT QUEBEC AND

M. Gagnon.

XXVIII
TABER, 1941–42
Lithograph
(The Carson Coll.)

Soyez
Prêts
L'ARMÉE
DOIT FINIR LA TÂCHE
IMPRIMÉ AU CANADA
PUBLIÉ POUR LE MINISTÈRE DE LA DÉFENSE NATIONALE PAR LE SERVICE DE L'INFORMATION, OTTAWA.

XXIX
Anonymous, 1940–41
Lithograph
(McGill University)

THE MEN ARE READY...

ONLY **YOU** CAN GIVE THEM WINGS

ISSUED BY THE DIRECTOR OF PUBLIC INFORMATION, OTTAWA.
UNDER THE AUTHORITY OF HON. JAMES G. GARDINER, MINISTER OF NATIONAL WAR SERVICES.

XXX
Anonymous, 1940–45
Lithograph
(M.G.)

ISSUED BY NATIONAL FILM BOARD, OTTAWA. PRINTED IN CANADA. NFB-2E

XXXI
A.B. STAPLETON, 1941–42
Lithograph
(N.A.C. C-90884)

XXXII
G.K. ODELL, 1941–42
Lithograph
(N.A.C. C-90887)

XXXIII
G.K. ODELL, 1943
Lithograph
The Ardiel Advertising Agency, Ltd., Toronto
(N.A.C. C-91837)

XXXIV
C.R. WILCOX, 1944–45
Lithograph
(N.A.C. C-91851)

JUSQU'AU BOUT!

Achetez des OBLIGATIONS DE LA VICTOIRE

No. 3 A.V.L.

XXXV
A.B. STAPLETON, 1940–45
Lithograph
(M.G. NMC 725038)
Photograph: William Kent

XXXVI
L.J. TREVOR, 1941–42
Lithograph
(The Carson Coll.)

L'ARTILLERIE DU FRONT INDUSTRIEL

Chacun À SON POSTE

TREVOR

PUBLIÉE PAR LE SERVICE DE L'INFORMATION, AVEC L'AUTORISATION DE L'HON. J. T. THORSON, MINISTRE DES SERVICES NATIONAUX DE GUERRE, OTTAWA.   IMPRIMÉE AU CANADA   17-4

XXXVII
Allan HARRISON, 1942–45
Silkscreen
(Harrison estate)

PRODUCE FOR

VICTORY

QUEBEC COMMITTEE FOR ALLIED VICTORY

XXXVIII
Anonymous, 1940–45
Lithograph
(The Carson Coll.)

Roll 'em Out!

Published and distributed under the authority and direction of the Director-General of Aircraft Production

XXXIX
J.E. SAMPSON, 1940–45
Lithograph
(N.A.C. C-91445)

XL
Hubert ROGERS, 1943
Lithograph
(N.A.C. C-103527)

ATTACK

1 ON ALL FRONTS

ISSUED BY WARTIME INFORMATION BOARD, OTTAWA. PRINTED IN CANADA

XLI
Anonymous, 1940–45
Lithograph
(N.A.C. C-87505)

NOTRE RÉPONSE

PRODUCTION MAXIMUM

Publié et distribué avec l'autorisation et sous la surveillance du Directeur Général de la Production Aéronautique.

Contribué à l'Oeuvre de Guerre du Canada par Canadian Pratt & Whitney Aircraft Company Limited

XLII
Charles FAINMEL, 1943–44
Lithograph
(N.A.C. C-87500)

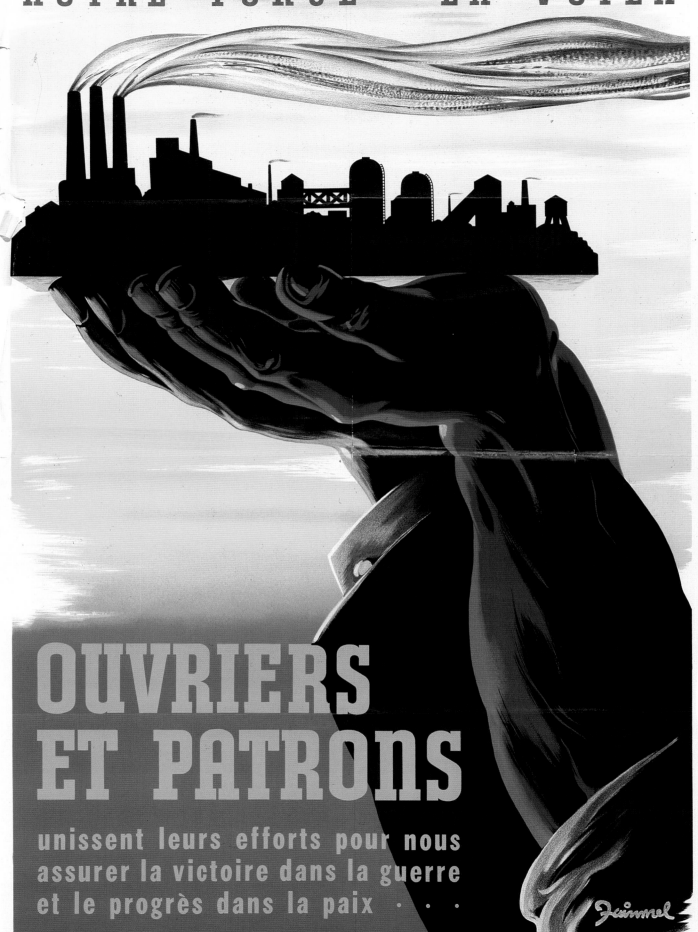

XLIII
Eric ALDWINCKLE, 1941–42
Lithograph
(The Carson Coll.)

IT'S OUR WAR

XLIV
TABER, 1943–44
Lithograph
(N.A.C. C-87437)

Issued by Wartime Information Board—Produced by National Film Board, Ottawa. Printed in Canada. Code No. —7E.

XLV
Harry MAYEROVITCH, 1943–44
Lithograph
(The Carson Coll.)

Je suis victime d'une
INDISCRÉTION

PUBLIÉ PAR LA COMMISSION D'INFORMATION EN TEMPS DE GUERRE—RÉALISÉ PAR L'OFFICE NATIONAL DU FILM, OTTAWA.   WIB 6F

XLVI
MORRIS, 1943–44
Lithograph
(The Carson Coll.)

Shoptalk may be Sabotalk

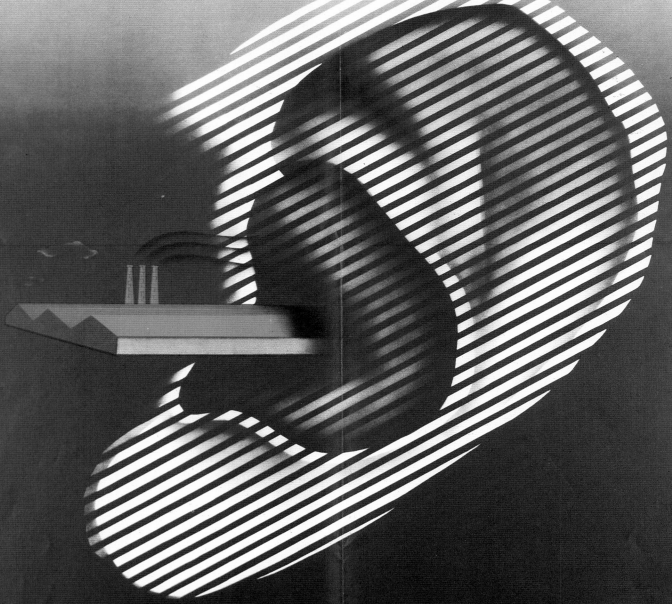

MORRIS

THE WALLS HAVE EARS

ISSUED BY WARTIME INFORMATION BOARD, OTTAWA PRINTED IN CANADA.   DESIGN, COURTESY WALLS HAVE EARS, ORGANIZATION

XLVII
Clair STEWART, 1941–42
Lithograph
(N.A.C. C-87534)

SEND THE BOYS *good* BOOKS AND MAGAZINES

GET IN TOUCH WITH YOUR LOCAL SALVAGE COMMITTEE | TEL.

ISSUED BY THE DIRECTOR OF PUBLIC INFORMATION FOR NATIONAL SALVAGE OFFICE, OTTAWA, UNDER AUTHORITY OF HONOURABLE J. T. THORSON, MINISTER OF NATIONAL WAR SERVICES. Printed in Canada

XLVIII
Harry MAYEROVITCH, 1943
Silkscreen
(N.A.C. C-115723)

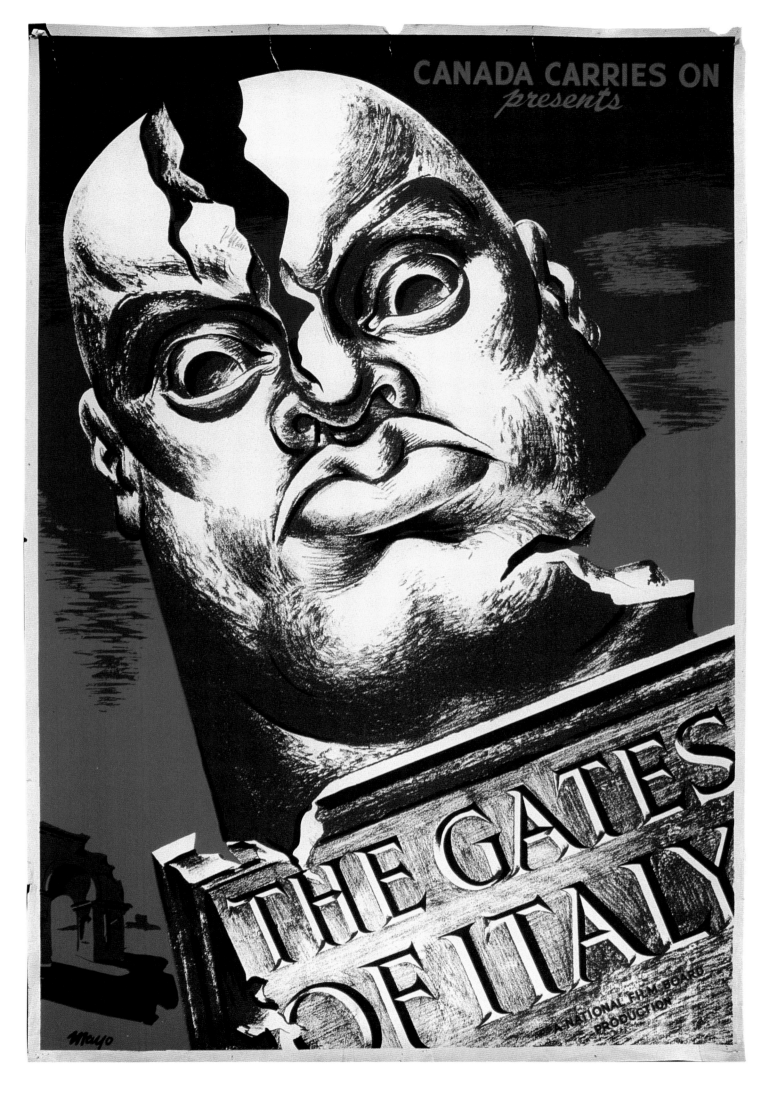

BLACK-AND-WHITE ILLUSTRATIONS

1. Anonymous, 1941–45
    Lithograph
    (N.A.C. C-91870)

2. After Edward PENFIELD, 1915–18
    Lithograph, 61 x 89
    (N.A.C. C-55113)

3. C.J. PATTERSON, 1915–18
    Lithograph, 52 x 70
    Flawson and Jones Ltd.
    (N.A.C. C-29568)

4. C.R. WILCOX, 1941–42
    Lithograph
    (The Carson Coll.)

5. Arthur KEELOR, 1915–18
    Lithograph, 61 x 92
    (The Carson Coll.)

6. Anonymous, 1915–18
    Lithograph, 63 x 95
    (The Carson Coll.)

7. Anonymous, 1915–18
    Lithograph, 69 x 106
    The Mortimer Co. Ltd., Ottawa
    (N.A.C. C-95377)

8. Anonymous, 1915–18
    Lithograph, 61 x 92
    (The Carson Coll.)

9. Anonymous, 1917–18
    Lithograph, 62 x 93
    Gazette Printing Co. Ltd., Montreal, Quebec
    (N.A.C. C-95380)

10. Anonymous, 1917–18
    Lithograph, 71 x 100
    The Mortimer Co. Ltd., Montreal, Quebec
    (N.A.C. C-95279)

11. Anonymous, 1917–18
    Lithograph, 67 x 104
    Montreal Litho. Co. Ltd.
    (N.A.C. C-95726)

12. Ken (Ken ROWELL?), 1941–45
    Lithograph
    (M.G. NMC-7511009)

13. Anonymous, 1941–42
    Lithograph
    (N.A.C. C-87132)

14. Anonymous, 1940–45
    Lithograph
    (N.A.C. C87516)

15. Anonymous, 1940–45
    Lithograph
    (N.A.C. C-87487)

16. Hubert ROGERS, c. 1942
    (N.A.C. C-87118)

17. Anonymous, 1941–42
    Lithograph
    (M.G. NMC-739231)

18. Anonymous, 1917–18
    Lithograph, 67 x 102
    (N.A.C. C-94392)

19. Anonymous, 1915–18
    Lithograph, 50 x 67
    Howell Litho., Hamilton
    (N.A.C. C-95277)

20. Ted HARRIS, 1941–45
    Lithograph
    (McGill University)

21. Arthur H. HIDER, 1915–18
    Lithograph, 68 x 103
    (The Carson Coll.)

22. Anonymous, 1917–18
    Lithograph, 68 x 105
    Montreal Litho Co. Ltd.
    (N.A.C. C-95385)

23. Anonymous, 1915–18
    Lithograph, 62 x 89
    Montreal Litho Co. Ltd.
    (N.A.C. 93227)

24. Anonymous, 1915–18
    Lithograph, 107 x 71
    The Mortimer Co. Ltd., Ottawa, Montreal, Toronto
    (N.A.C. C-95725)

79.

80.

81.

25. G.K. ODELL, 1941–45
Lithograph
(M.G. NMC-739220)

26. Anonymous, 1915–18
(also in a Yiddish version)
Lithograph, 69 x 104
Montreal Litho Co. Ltd.
(David M. Stewart Museum)

27. Hubert ROGERS, 1942–43
Lithograph
(N.A.C. C-87122)

28. W.H.T.?, 1915–18
Lithograph, 68 x 110
Howell Litho., Hamilton
(N.A.C. C-95288)

29. Anonymous, 1918
Lithograph, 61 x 91
(N.A.C. C-55111)

30. Anonymous, 1915–18
Lithograph, 45 x 60
(N.A.C. C-57359)

31. Anonymous, 1941–45
Lithograph
(N.A.C. C-87518)

32. Anonymous, 1917–18
Lithograph, 106 x 71
The Mortimer Co. Ltd., Ottawa, Montreal
(N.A.C. C-95376)

33. Anonymous, 1917–18
Lithograph, 106 x 71
The Mortimer Co. Ltd., Ottawa, Montreal
(N.A.C. C-95374)

34. Anonymous, 1941–45
Lithograph
(The Carson Coll.)

35. Harry MAYEROVITCH, 1943–44
Silkscreen
(N.A.C. C-115706)

36. Anonymous, 1915–18
Lithograph, 69 x 105
(M.G. NMC 7310615)

37. Anonymous, 1915–18
Lithograph, 61 x 91
(N.A.C. C-55107)

38. T.O.?, 1915–18
    Lithograph, 35 x 53
    J.J. Gibbons Ltd., Montreal
    (N.A.C. C-97745)

39. E. HENDERSON, 1915–18
    Lithograph, 71 x 106
    (N.A.C. C-139641)

40. Anonymous, 1915–18
    Lithograph, 56 x 84
    (The Carson Coll.)

41. Anonymous, 1915–18
    Lithograph, 61 x 91
    (N.A.C. C-97749)

42. E. HENDERSON?, 1915–18
    Lithograph, 46 x 62
    Howell Litho, Hamilton
    (N.A.C. C-95282)

43. Anonymous, 1940–41
    Lithograph
    (N.A.C. C-87545)

44. Anonymous, 1940–41
    Lithograph
    (N.A.C. C-87543)

45. Anonymous, 1917–18
    Lithograph, 68 x 105
    The Mortimer Co. Ltd., Ottawa
    (N.A.C. C-95386)

46. E. HENDERSON, 1915–18
    Lithograph, 46 x 62
    Howell Litho., Hamilton
    (N.A.C. C-95289)

47. Eric ALDWINCKLE, 1941–42
    Lithograph
    (The Carson Coll.)

48. P.H. SURREY, 1941–42
    Lithograph
    (The Carson Coll.)

49. Anonymous, 1941–45
    Lithograph
    (N.A.C. C-87482)

50. Anonymous, 1941–45
    Lithograph
    (N.A.C. C-91437)

51. Anonymous, 1940–41
    Lithograph
    (N.A.C. C-33442)

82.

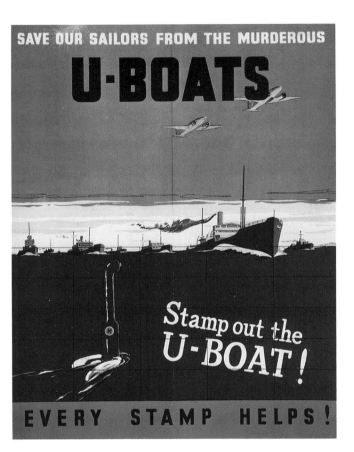

83.

84.

52. Clair STEWART, 1941–42
Lithograph
(N.A.C. C-87533)

53. Jac LEONARD, 1943–45
Lithograph
(The Carson Coll.)

54. R.?, 1917
Lithograph, 69 x 105
Heliothype Co. Ltd., Ottawa
(N.A.C. C-93224)

55. E. HENDERSON, 1917
Lithograph, 34 X 51
Howell Litho., Hamilton
(N.A.C. C-91459)

56. Anonymous, 1941–42
Lithograph
(The Carson Coll.)

57. Anonymous, 1915–18
Lithograph, 56 x 86
(N.A.C. C-93228)

58. NICHOL, 1941–42
Lithograph
(The Carson Coll.)

59. Anonymous, 1915–18
Lithograph, 66 x 102
Howell Litho., Hamilton
(N.A.C. C-95733)

60. W. BOOK?, 1941–42
Lithograph
(N.A.C. C-87464)

61. A.J. CASSON, 1941–42
Lithograph
(N.A.C. C-111083)

62. Anonymous, 1943–44
Lithograph
(N.A.C. C-87509)

63. N.F. ADAMSON, 1944
Lithograph
(N.A.C. C-91549)

64. Franklin ARBUCKLE, 1941–45
Lithograph
(The Carson Coll.)

65. W. BOOK, 1941–45
Lithograph
(N.A.C. C-91538)

66. Roger COUILLARD, 1943
    Lithograph
    (N.A.C. C-91865)

67. C. DAVID, 1915–18
    Lithograph, 62 x 92
    (N.A.C. C-95269)

68. F.J. FINLEY, 1941–45
    Lithograph
    (N.A.C. C-91467)

69. F.J. FINLEY, 1941–45
    Lithograph
    (N.A.C. C-91468)

70. Malcolm GIBSON, 1915–18
    Lithograph, 61 x 92
    (The Carson Coll.)

71. E. HENDERSON, 1915–18
    Lithograph, 46 x 62
    (The Carson Coll.)

72. A.L. McLAREN, 1941–42
    (After the portrait of a soldier by
    Charles Henry Biddle, of Calgary)
    Lithograph
    (N.A.C. C-91596)

73. A.L. McLAREN, 1943
    The Ardiel Advertising Agency Ltd., Toronto
    (N.A.C. C-91539)

74. F.L. NICOLET, 1915–18
    Lithograph, 90 x 61
    (N.A.C. 139637)

75. Hubert ROGERS, 1943
    Sketch
    (N.A.C. C-103300)

76. Hubert ROGERS, c. 1942
    Lithograph
    (N.A.C. C-87129)

77. Ron WHITE, 1941–45
    Lithograph
    (N.A.C. C-91866)

78. C.R. WILCOX, 1941–45
    Lithograph
    Edmond Cloutier, Ottawa
    (M.G. NMC-7510991)

79. Anonymous, 1915–18
    Lithograph, 67 x 102
    Montreal Litho. Co. Ltd.
    (N.A.C. C-95286)

85.

86.

MARINE MARCHANDE..........la quatrième arme

Après trois jours d'une lutte héroïque contre les attaques des sous-marins et des bombardiers ennemis, le capitaine Fred S. Slocombe, M.B.E., et son brave équipage réussirent à livrer aux autorités soviétiques le brise-glace MONTCALM, don du Canada à l'U.R.S.S.

87.

88.

90.

BIBLIOGRAPHY

Amstutz, Walter, ed. Who's Who in Graphic Art. Zurich: Amstutz and Herdeg Graphics Press, 1962.

Baynes, Ken. Art and Society One — War. Boston Book and Art Publisher, 1970.

Canadian War, The. January 23, 1915, p. 16.

Canadian Who's Who, The. Toronto: Trans-Canada Press, vol. 5, 1949–51.

Cantwell, John D. Images of War. British Posters, 1939–1945. Public Record Office, 1989.

Choko, Marc H. 150 ans de graphisme publicitaire au Québec. Archives nationales du Québec, 1987.

Choko, Marc H., and David L. Jones. Canadian Pacific Posters 1883–1963. Montreal: Méridien, 1988.

Collier, Sandra. War Posters. Mimeograph, n.d.

Comeau, André. Artistes plasticiens — Canada (Régime français et Conquête), Bas-Canada et le Québec. Montreal: Bellarmin, 1983.

Darracott, Joseph. The First World War in Posters. New York: Dover Publications, 1974.

Darracott, Joseph, and Belinda Loftus. Second World War Posters. London: Imperial War Museum, 1972.

Devaux, Simone, ed. La dernière guerre vue à travers les affiches. Paris: Atlas, 1978.

Dimson, Théo. Great Canadian Posters. Oxford University Press, 1979.

Doll, Maurice. 1993.

Dorais, Lucie. "Hubert Rogers." In Jim Burant et al., Un monument dans l'histoire. Ottawa: Archives nationales du Canada, 1991.

Evans, Gary. John Grierson and the National Film Board: The Politics of Wartime Propaganda. Toronto: University of Toronto Press, 1984.

Fainmel, Charles, and Henri Eveleigh. "The Proper Function of Advertising." Canadian Art, 4, no. 4 (1947): 157–159.

Gallo, Max. L'affiche. Miroir de l'histoire. Paris: Robert Laffont, 1973.

Greenhous, Brereton, and Stephen J. Harris. Canada and the Battle of Vimy Ridge, 9–12 April 1917. Department of Supply and Services Canada, 1992.

Halliday, Hugh A. Untitled (posters of World Wars I and II). Mimeograph, 1992.

Hardie, Martin, and Arthur K. Sabin. War Posters Issued by the Belligerent and Neutral Nations, 1914–1919. London: A. and C. Black Ltd., 1920.

Harper, Paula. War, Revolution and Peace. Propaganda Posters from the Hoover Institution Archives 1914–1945. c. 1975.

Harper, Russel J. Early Painters and Engravers in Canada. Toronto: University of Toronto Press, 1970.

Harrison, Allan. "Advertising Design in Canada." Canadian Art, 2, no. 3 (1945): 106–110.

Havlice, Patricia Pate. Index to Artistic Biography. 2 vols and supp. Metuchen: Scarecrow Press, 1973.

Hillier, Beavis. Histoire de l'affiche. Paris: Arthème Fayard, 1970.

Hunter, Sarah Lily, and Allen Shields McStay. All Together. World War I Posters of the Allied Nations. Dallas Historical Society, 1983.

Ilsley. Canada at War. A Message to Service Clubs. Mimeograph, 1942.

Judd, Denis. Posters of World War Two. London: Wayland, 1972.

Lismer, Arthur. "What's Wrong with Our Posters." The Montreal Standard, late 1942.

Lovell's Montreal Street Directory.

MacDonald, Colin S. A Dictionary of Canadian Artists. Ottawa: Canadian Paperbacks, 1977.

McMann, Evelyn de R. Royal Canadian Academy of Arts/Académie royale des arts du Canada. Exhibitions and Members 1880–1979. Toronto: University of Toronto Press, 1981.

McPherson Library, ed. Creative Canada. A Biographical Dictionary of Twentieth-Century Creative and Performing Artists. Toronto: University of Toronto Press, 1972.

Might Directories Ltd. The Ottawa City Directory.

— The Toronto City Directory.

Murray, Joan. Canadian Artists of the Second World War. Oshawa: The Robert McLaughlin Gallery, 1981.

91.

92.

"Posters." Canadian Business (September 1942): 124–125.

Rawls, Walton. Wake Up, America ! WWI and the American Poster. New York: Abbeville Press, 1988.

Rhodes, Anthony. Propaganda. The Art of Persuasion: World War II. New York: Chelsea House, 1976.

Richmond, Leonard. The Technique of the Poster. London: Pitman, 1933.

Rickards, Maurice. Posters of the First World War. New York: Walker and Co., 1968.

Robertson, Heather, ed. A Terrible Beauty: The Art of Canada at War. Toronto: J. Lorimer/Oshawa: Robert McLaughlin Gallery/Ottawa: National Museum of Man, 1977.

Rudolph, G.A. War Posters from 1914 through 1918 in the Archives of the University of Nebraska. Lincoln: University of Nebraska, 1990.

Stacey, Robert. The Canadian Poster Book. 100 Years of the Poster in Canada. Toronto: Methuen, 1982.

Stacey, Robert, and Mela Constantinidi. "The Poster in Canada." Canadian Collector, 14, no. 1 (1979): 11–15.

Stanley, Peter. What Did You Do in the War Daddy? A Visual History of Propaganda Posters. Melbourne: Oxford University Press, 1983.

Stephenson, H.E., and Carlton McNaught. The Story of Advertising in Canada. Toronto: Ryerson Press, 1940.

Tippet, Maria. Art at the Service of War. Canadian Art and the Great War. Toronto: University of Toronto Press, 1984.

"U.S.S.R. Posters Vividly Depict Fighting Spirit of Powerful Ally." Canadian Pacific Staff Bulletin, January 5, 1943.

Vézina, Raymond. "Canadian Posters in the Public Archives of Canada." IDEA, 31, no. 178 (1983): 52–69.

Wagg, Susan W. Percy Erskine Nobbs: Architect, Artist, Craftsman. Kingston: McGill-Queen's University Press/Montreal: McCord Museum, 1982.

Weill, Alain. L'affiche dans le monde. Paris: Aimery Somogy, 1984.

William, H.A. How England Raised an Army of Five Million Men and Floated Her Big War Loans. Montreal and Hamilton: The Canadian Poster Co. Ltd., n.d.

Wolff, Hennie, ed. The Index of Ontario Artists. Toronto: Visual Arts Ontario and Ontario Association of Art Galleries, 1978.

Wrede, Stuart. The Modern Poster. New York: The Museum of Modern Art, 1988.

Yanker, Gary. Prop Art. Paris: Planète, 1972.

Young and Rubicam Inc. How to Make Posters that Will Help Win the War. c. September 1942.

Young, Robert Williams. "Making the Truth Graphic: The Canadian Government's Home Front Information Structure and Programmes during World War. II." Ph.D. diss., University of British Columbia, 1978.

93.

Marc H. Choko is a professor in the faculty of design at l'*Université du Québec à Montréal*. He is a graduate of l'*Université de Montréal* in Architecture and Urban Development. He also has a Ph.D. in Urbanism from l'*Université de Paris VIII*. He authored many books on urban development and housing.

Mr. Choko has also shown a great interest in posters for the past thirty years. He was the curator of the exhibit *150 ans de graphisme publicitaire au Québec* and, in collaboration with David L. Jones, *Canadian Pacific Posters, 1883-1963*.

Marc H. Choko has published at *les Éditions du Méridien*:

– *Les grandes places publiques de Montréal*   (1987)
– *Affiches du Canadien Pacifique, 1883-1963*   (1988)
– *Canadian Pacific Posters, 1883-1963*   (1988)
– *Une cité-jardin à Montréal*   (1989)
– *The Major Squares of Montreal*   (1990)